Children's Rooms
and Play Yards

By the Editors of Sunset Books
and Sunset Magazine

Lane Books • Menlo Park, California

Foreword

The editors of *Sunset* Books and *Sunset* Magazine have always been interested in children's surroundings—both indoors and outdoors. In researching this subject, we have found that the recent direction has been toward more playthings which challenge young minds and bodies. For example, a single play structure might not only allow children to climb, hang, slide, and jump, but also let them imagine they are on a ship or in a fort, ghost town, or fire station. The ideas presented here, taken from articles published in *Sunset* Magazine, reflect this trend.

Children's Rooms and Play Yards, a complete updating of a title first published in 1960, is divided into two sections. The first portion deals with children's indoor living: bedrooms and playrooms, furniture, storage, and play equipment. The second section of the book covers outdoor play ideas, from sandboxes to geometric toys to elaborate playhouses. These ideas can be incorporated into a remodel or a new home, or they can be adapted to fit your present situation, and most can be made without difficulty right at home.

Edited by **Elizabeth Hogan**

PHOTOGRAPHERS

William Aplin: 60 bottom left; 77 top right. **Morley Baer:** 15 bottom. **Ernest Braun:** 19 bottom left, right; 20 top right; 27 top left, right; 51 bottom; 52 top; 76 bottom left; 85. **Steve Browning:** 50. **Glenn Christiansen:** 6; 12; 29 top; 33 top; 40 top; 42; 43; 46; 47; 55 bottom; 59 bottom left; 64; 68 top left, right; 69; 70 bottom left, right; 71 bottom left, right; 72; 73 bottom left; 83; 87 bottom left; 90; 91. **Robert Cox:** 32 bottom. **Dick Dawson:** 24 bottom. **Max Eckert:** 7. **Richard Fish:** 23; 24 top right; 26 bottom left, right; 27 bottom; 30 top, bottom right; 62 bottom; 79; 89 bottom left, right. **Joshua Freiwald:** 19 top left, right; 24 top left. **Walter Houk:** 51 top. **Frank Jensen:** 9; 22 bottom right; 82 bottom. **Roy Krell:** 20 top left. **Michael Lampton:** 35 bottom. **Edmund Y. Lee:** 20 bottom right; 23 bottom left; 29 bottom left; 30 bottom left; 88. **Leland Y. Lee:** 35 top left, right. **Richard E. Londgren:** 74. **Morris Studio:** 21 bottom. **Nelson/Zellers Photo Craft Co.:** 31 bottom left, right. **Don Normark:** 13; 16; 17; 18; 20 bottom left; 25 top left; 31 top; 52 bottom right; 54; 55 top left; 58 top, bottom right; 59 top, bottom right; 61; 71 top right; 77 bottom left, right; 84; 87 top left; 89 top right; 94; 95. **Phil Palmer:** 60 bottom right; 70 top left. **Photographic Illustrators:** 86. **Ray Piper:** 53. **Pete Redpath:** 14. **Ricco-Mazzuchi:** 21 top. **Tom Riley:** 25 bottom left; 73 top, bottom right; 76 top left, bottom right; 77 top left. **Martha Rosman:** 10; 11; 22 top left, right, bottom left; 25 right; 26 top left; 29 bottom left; 34; 52 bottom left; 62 top left, right; 63 top left, right; 68 bottom left, right; 71 top left; 87 top right, bottom right. **Douglas M. Simmonds:** 32 top right. **Darrow M. Watt:** 4; 15 top; 26 top right; 28; 33 bottom left, right; 36; 37; 38; 39; 40 bottom; 41; 44; 45; 48; 49; 55 top left; 56; 58 bottom right; 60 top left, right; 63 bottom left, right; 65; 66; 75; 80; 81; 82 top left, right; 92. **Roy O. Welch:** 32 top left. **R. Wenkam:** 8. **Paul Whitford:** 93. **George Woo:** 67.

Cover photograph by **Glenn Christiansen**. For details about this playhouse, see page 83.

Third Printing January 1972

CONTENTS

Children's Rooms   4

BEDROOMS, PLAYROOMS

Upstairs bedroom-playroom for two 6
Two rooms now sleep three 7
One playroom becomes two bedrooms . . . 8
Compact bedroom and a separate hideaway . 9
Built-ins make small room generous . . . 10
An attic hideaway 11
Playroom has outside, inside entrances . . 12
Three bedrooms open onto playroom . . 13
This playroom adjoins the bedroom . . . 14
Playrooms open to bedrooms, outdoors . . 15
A mud room for when it rains or snows . . 16

FURNITURE

Bunk beds that disappear 18
Drop-down bunks for overnight guests . . 19
Bunk beds save floor space 20
Bunks have climbing pole, landing platform . 21
This bedroom sleeps four 21
The bottom beds pull out 22
Beds up high leave play space below . . . 22
Bunking in a ship's cabin 23
Built-in counter-desks 24
Desks with overhead storage 25
Study tables that can grow 26

STORAGE

Ways to display and store toys 27
Shelf insert for toys, books 28
Simple plywood shelf for toys 29
Closets keep playthings out of sight . . . 29
Rolling toy storage drawers 30
Storage units are movable 30
Combination toy chests and benches . . . 31
Drawers store toys, clothing 32
Toy containers can be decorative 33
This train table folds up 34
Miniature railroad disappears 35
Slot cars slide under bed 35

INDOOR PLAY EQUIPMENT

Box blocks for storage or play 36
An indoor playhouse 39
Pine blocks for building 40
A wagon for toys and boys 40
Old-fashioned vehicles from scrap blocks . 41
"Anything" box keeps children busy . . . 42
Ferryboat does everything but float . . . 43
Play table and chairs that grow 44
Rocking toys for boys and girls 45
A doll house four stories tall 46
This doll house can go next door . . . 47
Modules make doll-sized apartments . . . 48

A Japanese doll house 49
An easel for two 50
Easel holds a paper roll 51
A place to display artwork 51
Wall ideas for drawings and displays . . . 52
A two-faced school board 53
Indoor exercise on rainy days 54
Household safety tips 55

Play Yards   56

SANDBOXES

Railroad ties frame sandboxes 58
Sandboxes can be almost anywhere 59
Sandboxes hold play equipment 60
A bottomless sandbox 61
Disappearing sandboxes 62

OUTDOOR PLAY EQUIPMENT

Triangles make giant geometric toys . . . 64
A goat cart or a rickshaw 65
Here you can swing, slide, or climb . . . 66
A garden landscaped for the children . . . 67
This swing is spill-proof 68
These swings are really old tires 68
Swings that hang from irregular branches . . 69
Back-yard play ideas 70
A doll house that floats 72
Water play on a hot day 73
An adjustable basketball hoop 74
A train table outdoors 75
Places to park the bicycles 76

PLAYHOUSES

A play structure full of surprises 78
Loft, deck highlight this A-frame 80
A-frame playhouse over old gym set 81
Combination playhouses and play yards . . 82
Up the ladder, down the fireman's pole . . 83
A playhouse for chinning and climbing . . 84
Kitchen appeals to girls, roof to boys . . 85
A two-story playhouse 86
Above-ground structures for outdoor play . . 87
A "tree" house without a tree 88
This house tucks into a fence corner . . . 89
A "floating" tree house 89
Front-yard tree house has to be presentable . 90
You go inside to go up 91

PARK EQUIPMENT

Obstacle course for a school play yard . . . 92
A small-scale Indian village 93
A children's park in the forest 94

Index   96

For information on this project, see page 36.

Children's Rooms

Children's rooms are highly individual—they differ with the age and needs of the child and the home facilities available. Some parents prefer a bedroom-playroom combination; some plan a playroom just off the bedroom; others allow for a completely separate play area. But whatever the location, a child's room must be adaptable, for the room will change as the child grows. When planning your child's room, here are some basic ideas to keep in mind:

■ Wall Surfaces. You will want a finish that is both washable and durable. Semi-gloss enamel is an ideal paint finish. Vinyl wallpaper is available decorated with children's designs; or a wall may be covered with cork or softboard and used as a giant bulletin board. Almost any smooth plaster or smooth wood wall can be made into a chalk board by covering it with special paint available at most paint stores. For a boy's room, wood paneling is a practical guard against rough wear.

■ Floor Surfaces. The best floors are resilient and easy to clean. Asphalt, vinyl, vinyl asbestos, linoleum, rubber, rubber plastic, and cork floor coverings provide a washable surface and will withstand heavy wear. Because children spend so much time on the floor, carpeting may be preferred. Tufted kitchen carpets are available in plaids, prints, bright colors, and tweeds. Indoor-outdoor carpeting will withstand rough treatment and may be purchased in a 9 by 12-foot size, in 12-inch self-adhesive tiles, or laid wall to wall. Nylon shag carpeting (treated for static) with a 1½ to 2-inch pile provides warmth and is very easy to clean. It is also sold in self-adhesive square yard tiles. Area rugs, available in a wide range of bright colors, shapes, sizes, and materials, add color accent and individuality to a room. Furry nylon rugs come in whimsical shapes.

■ Sleeping Space. A bed is nearly always the biggest piece of furniture in a child's room. If floor space is limited, there are several space-saving types of beds. Bunk beds are probably the most common; however, keep in mind that the upper bed can be difficult to make and may be too warm, unless the room is well ventilated. There are also beds that fold up against the wall or are arranged in such a way to occupy a minimum amount of space.

■ Work Space. A table, desk, or counter is needed by the school-age child for working on hobbies, artwork, and homework. If a room is shared, each child should have an area of his own. Make the work space as generous as possible, as children like to spread out.

■ Storage Space. Children tend to have large numbers of toys and collections, and if their rooms are to remain fairly organized, there should be plenty of storage space. Open shelves are good—everything is out on display, easily reached, and easily returned to place.

■ Lighting. Ceiling-attached or recessed fixtures should cast fairly even light over the entire room. Portable lamps are not always advisable for infants and toddlers as they fall over easily, and the outlets are intriguing to curious small children. Outlets can be covered with blank face plates in the nursery. For the school-age child, a student lamp, gooseneck lamp, or tensor light works well.

Upstairs bedroom-playroom for two

Although two young boys share one large bedroom-playroom, they can also have some privacy. An accordion-folding wood partition which runs on a track along the ceiling beam divides the room into two. Each end of the room has a large window, its own built-in storage cabinet and closet, and a hallway access to the bath.

When the partition is open, there is plenty of space for special projects. Wall-to-wall carpeting keeps the noise level down (this is a second-story room) and makes cleanup easy. The bed's headboard (foreground in photograph at left) and shelves and cases against the wall are handy places to store and display toys.

BUILT-IN CABINET, *adjustable shelves hold books, toys. Cork board contains news clips, reminders.*

LARGE PLAY AREA *can be partitioned into two bedrooms. Each section has window, storage units.*

STORAGE UNIT *converts to desk by removing shelf, doors. Note cabinet has no bottom shelf.*

Two rooms now sleep three

The room shown in the two photographs below is the original bedroom in a relatively small house. By adding the room shown at right, with access through two large doorways, three small children were given private sleeping quarters that convert into one generous play area. A wealth of storage places encourages neatness. Carpeting on the floor and acoustical tile on the ceiling help to cut down the noise.

Architect: Donald Goldman.

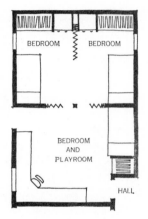

NEW ROOM *can be divided into two bedrooms by folding door that pulls out from between dressers.*

L-SHAPED COUNTER, *shelves, toy bin on casters provide plenty of work, play, storage space.*

CLOSET *was shortened to gain alcove for third bed, has blackboard door. Note storage overhead.*

One playroom becomes two bedrooms

In this convertible children's room, space opens up into a large playroom or partitions off into smaller private sleeping quarters. An accordion-folding door stacks into a boxlike structure between the two desks. These desks run the full width of each half and serve as headboards for the freestanding beds. Above the windows are bookshelves; at the opposite end of each section is a closet with a built-in chest of drawers. Each sleeping area was designed with its own entryway into the hall.

    Architect: Edward Sullam.

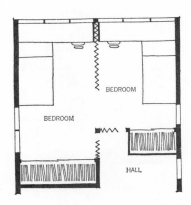

FOLDING DOOR *closes for privacy. Curtained windows above counter reduce glare on desk surface.*

SEPARATE ENTRIES *provide easy access to hall; closets have double clothes rods, built-in shelves.*

Compact bedroom and a separate hideaway

The boy's bedroom pictured at right has built-in furniture with little or no space underneath to collect dust and the usual tangle of toys, books, and clothing. Posters and pin-ups can be tacked to the wood paneling on the walls. The desk is large enough for hobby projects. Plenty of daylight is provided through the window and the skylight.

The hideaway (shown below) is simply a loft above the children's bath and closets. Designed to satisfy the desire of children to get off alone or with a close friend, it overlooks the family room.

Architect: Ronald Molen.

LOFT *gets plenty of daylight through clerestory. Toy chest against back wall doubles as bench.*

BUILT-IN LADDER *leads to hideaway. Side of loft is high enough so children won't fall over.*

CARPETING *is coved under bunk for easier cleaning. Permanent ladder helps to support upper bunk.*

Built-ins make small room generous

Although this room is only 8½ by 11½ feet, it accommodates a built-in desk, a swing-out bed, and storage units. Light-colored walls add a sense of openness to this small room. During the day and early evening the room is used for study and play, and the bed functions as a couch. For changing or making the bed, it swings out on five casters into the room; for sleeping it rolls back into its position against the wall. The padded bolster above the bed is attached to the wall. At the head of the bed is a fixed shelf covered with linoleum for toy display and storage.

Along the opposite wall is a built-in unit with a counter top made of ¾-inch plywood, also covered with linoleum. The drawers are standard modular units available at department or furniture stores or at lumberyards. Additional storage space is provided in the two custom-built drawers underneath the bed and on the two shelves above the bed.

Architect: Peter Gray Scott.

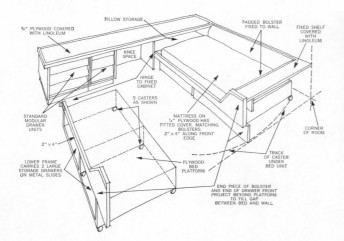

BED SWINGS OUT *into room for changing or making, is rolled back against wall for sleeping.*

MATTRESS COVER, *pillow slip, bolsters convert bed into sofa while room is used for study, play.*

An attic hideaway

Unused attic space in this house was put to good use as a children's retreat and occasional bunk room. With a roll-back roof, it is an exciting place to spend a sunny afternoon or a clear evening watching the sky.

The hideaway is 8 by 12 feet and 6 feet high. It has a 2½-foot-wide shelf long enough for two mattresses placed end to end. You enter on a ladder-stair from a bedroom below.

The roof section rolls open on wheels along an aluminum track. It's driven by a long metal screw powered by a ⅕-horsepower motor. The closed roof is weatherproof. (Check with your local building inspector before trying this.)

OUTSIDE, *sliding roof section straddles roof ridge.*

CLOSED ROOF *is weatherproof. Intercom (above bed) is for communicating with the world below.*

ROOF SECTION *rolls open on wheels along track. Wood paneling adds warmth to small area.*

Playroom has outside, inside entrances

The owners of this house wanted a separate play and work room for their children, but one which would relate to the children's bedroom. Their solution was to convert a second-story sundeck over the kitchen into a playroom and connect it to the garden and outdoor play area by a railed spiral staircase. The children can enter their playroom directly from their bedroom (see floor plan) or from the outside. From the kitchen below, their mother can hear confrontations that get overly noisy and watch comings and goings on the spiral stairs.

Sky-turned windows and a 12-foot-high ceiling give the playroom an airy and spacious feeling. Underneath the windows is a cavelike area for storing large toys. A desk is built in at each end of a wall-to-wall counter. Above the counter are shelves for storing play items and books.

Architect: Sanford Pollack.

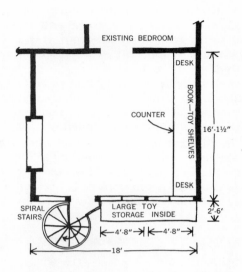

DESKS *are built in at each end of counter. Large toys are stored in open area under windows.*

SPIRAL STAIRS *give children direct access to outside play area, eliminate trooping through house.*

Three bedrooms open onto playroom

The children's wing in this house consists of three small sleeping rooms, a compartmented bath, a playroom, and a storage closet. Though the bedrooms are small, the high-beamed ceilings and a generous use of glass give a sense of spaciousness. A folding bed is kept in the storage closet so that it can be easily placed in one of the bedrooms to accommodate an overnight guest.

The playroom contains a large deep cupboard for storing toys and games. It also has a bookcase and a well-lighted center table so the room can double as a study hall. The vinyl floors and plastic laminate surfaces in the bedrooms and playroom are sturdy and easy to maintain.

Architects: John Rushmore and Associates.

PLAYROOM *is well lighted for games and study; open space, moveable furniture allow room for boys' roughhousing.*

CLOTHES CHUTE *behind louvered doors ends on laundry level below.*

This playroom adjoins the bedroom

ADJUSTABLE SHELVES *on vinyl-covered wall panels store equipment. Architect: Paul M. Wolff.*

PLYWOOD SECTIONS *with interlocking grooved edges make an assortment of play furniture.*

WIDE COUNTER, *pull-out drawers, built-in and adjustable shelves keep bedroom organized.*

Playrooms open to bedrooms, outdoors

TWO SMALL BEDROOMS *open onto spacious playroom. On lower level of hillside house, bedrooms look directly into hill, get daylight through sliding glass wall opening to playroom. Architect: Clement Chen.*

SLIDING DOORS *behind blackboard panels close off bedrooms. Glass doors at either end of playroom open to the outside. Mail box is used as clothes bin, alphabet box as toy chest. Architect: Jacob Robbins.*

A mud room for when it rains or snows

A mud room solves the problems created when you live in a rainy or snowy climate and have children rushing in and out of the house. This one is unusually well organized and complete.

Located between a heated garage and the kitchen, the mud room is accessible from the garage, the kitchen, and an outdoor deck. It has a half bath alongside, plus a space for a large freezer, handy to both car and kitchen.

One large closet with sliding doors holds camping and picnic gear, and there's an even larger open closet (plus additional wall hooks) for damp boots and jackets that need air circulation to dry. Recessed duckboards in the floor take care of the muddy boot problem, and the tile floor is easily mopped. A 4-inch drain pipe is underneath the concrete floor and catches the water from the duckboards.

Architects: Edwin B. Crittenden and Kenneth Maynard of Crittenden, Cassetta, Wirum & Cannon.

OPEN CLOSET *stores most-used sports equipment, heavy clothing. Lower shelves can double as benches for removing wet clothing. Wall hooks and perforated panel hold jackets and boots for quick drying.*

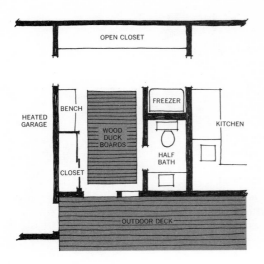

LOW WALL FAUCET *is for hosing concrete floor, filling dog's bowl. Animals also use mud room.*

TILED FLOOR *with recessed duckboards for removing wet, muddy boots has drain underneath.*

LARGE CABINET *has adjustable shelves for neatly storing camping, hiking, picnicking equipment.*

Bunk beds that disappear

These folding bunk beds made it possible to put two beds in an 8½ by 11½-foot room and have leftover space for play and two study desks.

To secure the beds to the wall, you'll need to expose two wall studs the same distance apart as the length of the mattresses you will use, plus 3¼ inches (to allow for the folding frames). This usually means adding 1 by 4 or 2 by 4 blocks to the existing studs, or adding a stud to the wall. The two uprights secured to these studs are 14½ inches wide for the lower 28½ inches; then they step back to 9 inches so the outer uprights can pivot up onto them.

Use any joinery desired on the bunk framing. Bolt the two bunk frames to the wall uprights and, with the bunks level, attach the two 5-inch-wide front uprights temporarily with small bolts. Swing the whole assembly up into the closed position to see if everything fits. Then install ⅝-inch-thick bolts.

For the counterweights, cable and pulleys are available at marine supply stores and sash weights at lumberyards. Attach the cables to the front uprights so they will run level to the pulleys when the bunks are folded up. Adjust the spring tension to your liking. Then panel the exposed wall with ¼-inch hardboard or plywood.

Design: Paul J. Peterson.

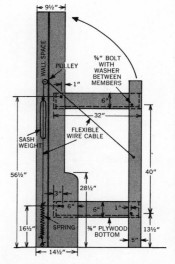

COUNTERWEIGHTS *and springs raise and lower beds; all wood parts are made of ¾-inch plywood.*

STURDY BEDS *are secured to wall studs by floor to ceiling uprights, have extra strong bottoms.*

BEDS SWING UP *against wall freeing entire floor space for varied activities of young boys.*

Drop-down bunks for overnight guests

BULLETIN BOARD-BUNK BED COMBINATION *is fastened to wall by overhead hook. When dropped down, bunk is held in place by strong hinges, chains. Architects: Fisher-Friedman Associates.*

UPPER BUNK, *attached to wall by side hook, is held on chain and bar when folded down. Steps are dowels anchored in wall (see photo at left). Underside of bunk has bulletin-board surface. Architect: Henrik Bull.*

Bunk beds save floor space

TOP BUNK *was placed higher than normal to leave more space below for book shelves and bedding (behind doors). Architects: Liebhardt & Weston.*

WALL LADDER *is out of way so lower bed is easy to make. Drawers have hinged tops, can be used as steps for making top bunk. Architect: David Tucker.*

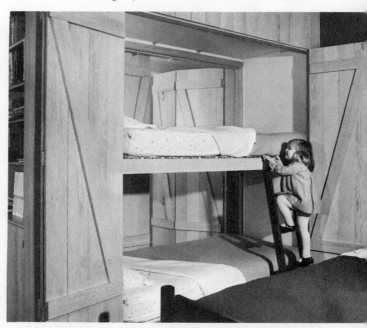

SUSPENDED FROM BEAM, *bunk can be removed without marring walls. Head rests on ledger strip, foot on shelf frame. Design: Dr. Leonard Nevler.*

BUNK BEDS *open into bedroom on one side, hallway on the other. Bifolding doors can be closed halfway for guard rail. Architect: Richard Sundeleaf.*

Bunks have climbing pole, landing platform

Two small boys share this bunk bed in a tiny bedroom off their play area. A great space saver, the bed fits neatly along one wall of a room which is roughly 9 feet square.

The upper bunk, reached by a ladder, is really a mattress atop a platform. The bottom bed is freestanding; it rolls in and out on casters like an ordinary bed.

A box frame of 2 by 4's was attached to the walls on three sides and supported by a 4 by 4 post on the outer side. Inch-diameter dowels, set into the post at suitable intervals, form a ladder.

A pair of 2 by 2's, lying at right angles to the frame, supports the ¾-inch-thick plywood platform that holds the mattress. To prevent anyone from falling out of bed, a 1 by 4 crossbar was affixed to vertical dowels set into the 2 by 2's; this same railing lifts out for bed making.

The landing platform at the top of the ladder is built of 1 by 2's.

Design: Eugene A. Kubly.

UPPER BED, *reached by dowel ladder, rests on wood platform; lower bed is freestanding.*

This bedroom sleeps four

Two bunks and two freestanding beds nicely accommodate four young boys in a relatively small bedroom (11 feet by 12 feet 10 inches). All four beds are standard twin size. The two bunks are placed end to end against one wall atop a block of storage drawers 36 inches deep by 39 inches high. Each drawer is 3 feet wide and 30 inches in depth; the 6 top drawers are 8½ inches high, and the two bottom drawers are 11 inches high.

A two-section safety rail runs alongside the bunks from wall to wall and can be removed for making the beds. A shutter across the lower half of the high window keeps drafts off the beds. Each bunk has a wall reading light.

The two lower beds, in recesses on either side of the storage drawers, have head room for small children, or the head can be at the outer end. The beds slide in and out of the recess.

The wall opposite the beds contains a desk, reading lamp, and movable shelves on perforated hardboard.

Design: Bernard J. Schmidt.

TWIN BUNKS *run along one wall, top a massive 6½-foot-wide block of storage drawers, have protective rail. Floor beds are freestanding.*

The bottom beds pull out

These two versions of the trundle bed were designed specifically for small bedrooms. The lower bed provides a place for an overnight guest and tucks away during the day to free the floor space. The upper bunk mattress is about 3 feet off the floor, so it is easy to make and change the bed. The lower bed glides on smooth end boards out on the cork floor. Toe space along bottom boards is for pulling the bed out and getting to the top.

The beds are constructed of solid redwood finger-jointed panels (you can use plywood). The upper bunks are 6 feet 4 inches long and 3 feet wide; the lower ones are a few inches shorter. The mattresses are 4-inch pin core rubber foam and rest on a plywood base.

Design: John Kapel.

CUTOUTS along bottom serve as steps to top bed, as hand-holds for pulling lower bed out.

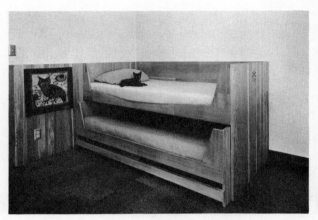

UPPER BUNK is attached to wall. Toe space above bottom board is for getting to top, pulling bed out.

Beds up high leave play space below

SUSPENDED BED with dowel ladder at foot frees floor space. Design: Donald M. Kobrin.

ANCHORED to two walls, 5-foot-high bed frees floor for dresser-desk, play. Architect: Ronald Molen.

Bunking in a ship's cabin

The young boy living in this room enjoys all the romance of living in a ship's cabin. His bunk is a single (twin-size) bed in a structure that is braced from the wall and hung from the ceiling. The space under the bed contains drawers for clothing and a second pull-out bed with a foam mattress. To make vacuuming easier, the only furniture legs that touch the floor in the room are attachable ones that brace the drawer bed when it's pulled out.

Design: James A. Douglass.

CABINLIKE BUNK *is suspended a foot above floor; it has drawer bed, other drawers for clothing.*

LADDER *of 4 by 4 post and staggered 1¼-inch dowels is attached to wall at foot of bed.*

SUPPORTING LEGS *of pull-out bed screw into sockets placed at corners of the frame.*

Built-in counter-desks

BUILT-IN COUNTER-DESK *has ample storage drawers. Architects: Fisher-Friedman Associates.*

CABINETS *support working counter-desk angled to fit corner of room. Design: Eduardo Tirella.*

COUNTER *(2½ by 8½ feet) can be used for sewing or as a desk. For typing, a special shelf at the side is set 3 inches lower than the counter. Architect: Sidney Snyder of Vladimir Ossipoff & Associates.*

Desks with overhead storage

LAMINATED WOOD COUNTER *has storage above. Architects: Bennie M. Gonzales & Associates.*

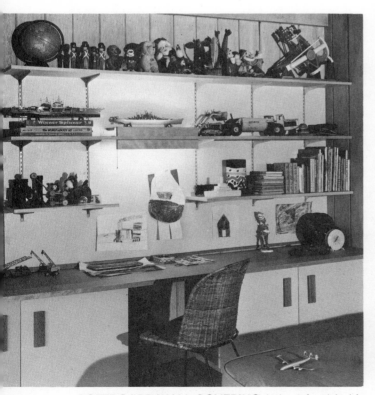

SOFTBOARD WALL COVERING *(4 by 8 feet) holds shelves supported by metal tracks, is for pinups.*

FULL-LENGTH METAL STRIPS *hold adjustable shelves, desk surface. Architect: John C. Hill.*

Study tables that can grow

WRITING SURFACE, *shelves are supported by dowels threaded through pole supports.*

PLYWOOD BOXES *with aluminum corner posts and piece of 18-inch-wide shelving make desk.*

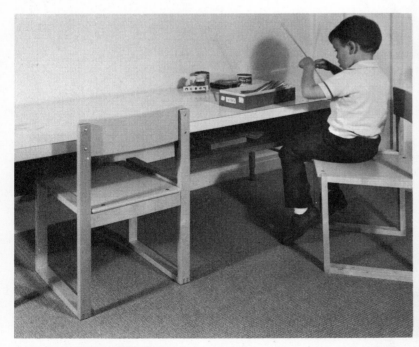

PLAY-WORK TABLE *has plastic laminate top, wood storage shelf below, and steel frame with telescoping legs. Table legs can lengthen—inner member slips down, screw secures it. Design: Robert Pottberg.*

Ways to display and store toys

WOODEN BOXES *glued in random pattern to sheet of plywood fastened to wall display and store toys.*

WALL-HUNG CASES *show off collection of dolls, horses. Sliding glass doors keep toys dust free.*

OPEN SHELVES *surrounding window encourage toy organization. Those at sides are adjustable; the ones below serve as a bench. When children are grown, shelves can be bookcases. Architect: Harry Saunders.*

Shelf insert for toys, books

This shallow shelf, assembled and then positioned in the wall, provides storage and display space for magazines and toys. The sides and vertical dividers are 1 by 6-inch clear fir, resawn to $3\frac{7}{8}$ inches wide; shelves are $\frac{1}{2}$-inch stock, similarly trimmed. The two central verticals are rabbeted for a $\frac{1}{2}$-inch-thick pin-up board.

The completed unit, about $2\frac{1}{2}$ feet high and 4 feet wide, fits in an opening spanning three stud intervals. If the wall is not load-bearing, a single 2 by 4 top and bottom and the existing studs at either side can suffice as rough framing. In a bearing wall, you will need a double 2 by 4 header and additional 2 by 4 vertical supports at the sides, both above and below the single bottom 2 by 4.

Prime the assembled shelf and slide it into the wall opening; nail it to the framing. Nail on the trim and prime; then enamel the entire unit. Force dowels into $\frac{3}{4}$-inch-deep holes in the outside verticals, then reverse them $\frac{1}{4}$ inch into shallower holes on opposite sides.

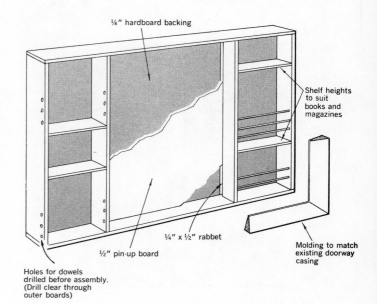

⅛" hardboard backing

Shelf heights to suit books and magazines

¼" x ½" rabbet

½" pin-up board

Molding to match existing doorway casing

Holes for dowels drilled before assembly. (Drill clear through outer boards)

COMPARTMENTED SHELF, *inserted in wall over bed, keeps calendar, books, mementoes close at hand. Pin-up board, ½ inch thick with ⅛-inch backing, can be pulled out and replaced when badly pocked.*

Simple plywood shelf for toys

These wall-hung shelves are ideal for displaying toys. Made of ½-inch overlaid plywood, each 3½-inch-wide shelf has a plywood backing that projects upward to make it easy to mount on the wall after it has been assembled. The ½ by ¾-inch walnut trim around the sides and front is applied with contact cement so that no nails will show.

PLYWOOD LEDGE *with walnut trim is mounted on wall to store and display toy vehicles.*

Closets keep playthings out of sight

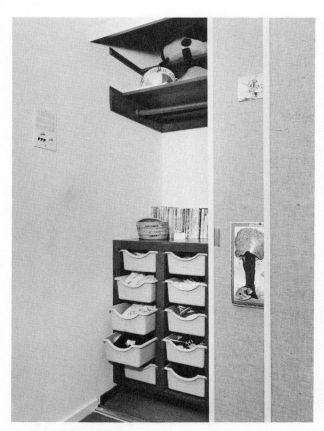

PLASTIC-BIN DRAWERS, *shelf keep closet organized. Architects: Ernest J. Kump Associates.*

SEPARATE CLOSETS *have adjustable shelves for storing playthings. Architect: Richard Sundeleaf.*

Rolling toy storage drawers

These handy toy storage chests are quite simple to build and can be located in the kitchen, family room, playroom, or bedroom. The sides and bottoms are ½-inch fir plywood with plain butt joints secured with glue and nails; the bottoms are reinforced with ¾-inch boards on the underside. The fronts are ¾-inch ash plywood. The top edge of each front was grooved deeply to serve as a finger-pull (the same is true of the drawers directly above them), eliminating any need for cabinet pulls or handles.

Each box rolls out in any direction on four spherical, 2½-inch-diameter casters mounted on the bottom. The toy boxes are tapered (about two inches narrower in the back than the front), so children do not have to take perfect aim to put them back in place. Each rolls in easily.

Design: Harper Poulson.

PLYWOOD CHESTS *roll in and out on casters, neatly store building blocks, other small toys.*

Storage units are movable

LARGE STORAGE BINS *glide on casters, fit under window seat. Architect: Richard Sundeleaf.*

TOY CHEST *rolls out from underneath TV set. Cut-out is handle. Architects: Tucker & Shields.*

Combination toy chests and benches

You can make or buy storage chests which will keep play equipment out of sight and also provide additional seating. The chest shown at right sits on casters and can be easily moved around the room. Each of the four drawers has a cutout for a handle. A covered cushion on top of the wooden structure makes seating more comfortable.

The bench shown below, designed so that the room could be converted quickly from a playroom to a center for entertaining, is angled to fit the wall and contains two storage bins. The bins have koa plywood tops and are faced with koa wood; however, other wood can be used. Low enough so children are able to fetch and put away their toys, the chests have pull-up lids, and the hinged tops rest against the wall. Pads can be placed on top of the bins, when they are closed, to adjust the sitting height for adults.

TOY CHEST *has storage drawers, cushioned seat, roll-around casters. Design: Dr. Leonard Nevler.*

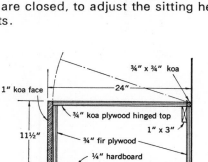

¾" x ¾" koa

1" koa face

24"

¾" koa plywood hinged top

1" x 3"

11½"

¾" fir plywood

¼" hardboard

2½"

2" x 3"s

SECTION VIEW

EXTRA SEATING *is provided by closed bins. Pads raise sitting height. Architect: George T. Johnson.*

HINGED TOPS *are low enough for small children; bins are deep enough for various-sized toys.*

Drawers store toys, clothing

ROLL-OUT DRAWERS *have rubber-tired wheels mounted on sides. Guides, stops on underside of bed keep drawers in position. Design: R. O. Osburn.*

STURDY PLASTIC BINS *slide along grooves notched in plywood verticals. Sliding doors close to conceal storage unit. Architect: Robert S. Grant.*

GRADUATED DRAWERS *with cut-out handles hold clothes, toys. Built-in unit also includes shelves, closets, lots of space to encourage youngsters to be neat and orderly. Architect: Kermit L. Darrow.*

Toy containers can be decorative

Children may be more willing to put their toys away if storage units are fun and attractive. Toy containers can also liven up the room. To make the boxes shown at right, select a sturdy cardboard carton (if its top is open, glue it securely back together). To decorate, paste a bold design of wallpaper or gift paper over the sides and top. Cut the lid about 4 inches down from the top in front, slanting up to the rear corners on the sides. Reinforce the cut edges with adhesive-backed cloth tape.

The fiber drums pictured below are inexpensive, roomy, durable, and easily decorated with latex paint, wallpaper scraps, or self-adhesive vinyl plastic. Some drums come with metal bottoms and snap-on lids (the ones shown here have had the snaps removed). When used during the summer as moth-proof storage for clothing, they can become corner or bedside tables.

These drums can be purchased in many variations of diameter and height. Those that seem most practical for toy storage are 15½ inches in diameter, varying in height from 14 to 32 inches. To find where you can purchase these units, look in the yellow pages of your telephone directory under "Barrels and Drums."

CARDBOARD CARTONS *attractively decorated with wallpaper or gift paper hold toys, small people.*

FIBER DRUMS *can be decorated with wallpaper, paint, or vinyl plastic and used as storage containers, end or corner tables. Large enough to hold toys, bulky items, drums have metal lids for long-term storage.*

This train table folds up

Designed to fit into a boy's small bedroom, this train table fits snugly against the wall when not in use. Sliding bolts in the upper corners hold it upright, but it can be swung down onto its hinged legs quickly (it straddles the bed) to use.

The track and roadbed are nailed on a piece of 4 by 8-foot plywood, edged with 1 by 6's to keep rolling stock from falling off in case of an accident and to protect the track and switches when against the wall.

The board is hinged to a 2 by 6-inch shelf fastened to the wall by brackets and attached at each end to a vertical 1 by 12. Felt backing hides the wiring and provides an attractive surface when the board is upright. The felt is held on with snap tape, so it's easily opened for repairs. The control panel is fastened on a board backed with fiberboard, with the wiring between.

Architect: J. M. Thornton.

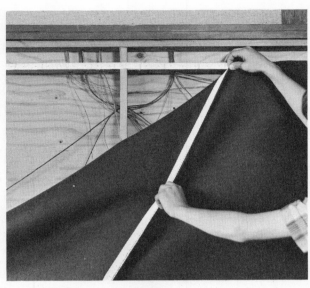

CONTROL PANEL WIRES *fan out under a covering of dark felt edged with snap tape for easy removal.*

PLYWOOD TRAIN TABLE *(4 by 8 feet) is edged with 1 by 6's to keep track and roadbed in place.*

SLIDING BOLTS *in upper corners secure train table against wall. Felt backing conceals wires.*

Miniature railroad disappears

TRAIN BOARD folds down on butt hinges from 15-inch recess, is supported by two legs, shelf ledge.

FOLDED UP, table is part of wall. Back is used for picture display. Architect: Ronald A. Ettinger.

Slot cars slide under bed

LARGE PLYWOOD SHEET holds roadbed for slot cars. Small casters at each corner allow children to roll entire board under bed for storage. Decorative elements are paper and are not attached to plywood.

Box blocks for storage or play

These modular boxes stack together to form bookcases, room dividers, wall storage cabinets, and desks. Or they can make caves, tunnels, airplanes, houses, and trains. The 16-inch cube boxes are easy and inexpensive to build. Sturdy but lightweight, they have ¼-inch plywood sides (lauan plywood is excellent), joined together with an aluminum "corner post"—item #3006 of the "do-it-yourself" aluminum.

You can build the boxes with hand tools, but a radial-arm or table saw eases the job. Cut the side panels an even 16 inches high but only 15¼ inches wide. Cut the bottoms *approximately* 15⅜ inches square (before cutting, double check this dimension on an assembled box). Glue sides into corner posts with white glue or a wall paneling mastic. Secure the bottom to the sides with glue and ¾-inch escutcheon pins. File down sharp corner post edges.

Some of these boxes have large holes—two round or rectangular holes in opposite sides, or a round hole in one side. The holes, cut before or after assembly, make the boxes more fun, yet they're still usable for storage. If necessary, strengthen plywood above the holes with strips of hardwood, glued to the inside.

The train shown on page 38 transforms three of the boxes into a mobile toy. It consists of three simple dollies on which boxes and children ride. The engine slips down over the front of one box. For the dollies, use flat-base casters with rubber or plastic wheels. Attach a wood edging to the engine's dolly, so the engineer can use his feet to steer or pedal without shifting his box. Connect the dollies with short pieces of rope. The train can be pushed or pulled with a knotted rope attached to the bell cord hole.

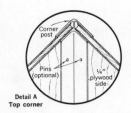

Detail A
Top corner

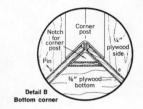

Detail B
Bottom corner

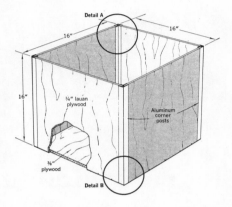

GLUE PLYWOOD SIDES *into aluminum corner posts. Use white glue liberally, a mastic sparingly.*

CUT ALUMINUM *at same time you cut plywood. Radial-arm or table saw will do the job quickly, easily.*

LIGHTWEIGHT BOXES *can easily be moved around by children; holes make boxes more interesting.*

ROUND HOLES *on two sides of boxes placed end to end make fine tunnels for young explorers.*

STACKED BOXES *can be used as room dividers, storage cabinets, or play furniture.*

Box blocks (con't)

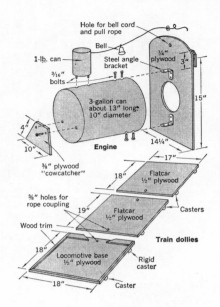

Hole for bell cord and pull rope

Bell

1-lb. can

¼" plywood

3"

Steel angle bracket

³⁄₁₆" bolts

3-gallon can about 13" long 10" diameter

15"

4"

10"

14¼"

Engine

⅜" plywood "cowcatcher"

17"

Flatcar ½" plywood

18"

Casters

⅜" holes for rope coupling

Wood trim

19"

Flatcar ½" plywood

Train dollies

18"

Locomotive base ½" plywood

Rigid caster

18"

Caster

TRAIN *made from three boxes tracks best with two non-swiveling casters on rear of engine's dolly.*

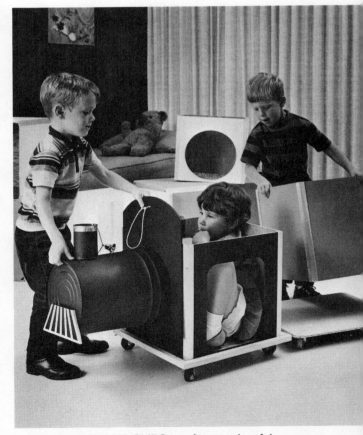

ENGINE SIMPLY SLIPS *on front side of box, can be stored inside box when not in use.*

An indoor playhouse

This curious piece of furniture can be used as a cupboard, a marionette theater, a submarine, or a toy box, or it can simply provide storage space for dolls, books, and toys. Children can hide in one section and still look at the outside world through a periscope. A ladder and a roped-in deck topside satisfy their desire to climb. A rolling toy box allows them to move their toys around.

Construction is simple and straightforward. Sides, top, bottom, door, and shelves are of ¾-inch plywood. The back is ¼-inch plywood, and the ladder is vertical grain fir. For the railing on top, use 2-inch dowels and a 1 by 2 fir strip, or fancier turned uprights in place of dowels. You'll also need a length of rope for the railing, 4 strap hinges for the toy boxes, 4 cabinet hinges and 2 magnetic catches for the bench and door, and 8 casters that measure 2 to 3 inches top to bottom. A short length of traverse rod holds the curtains.

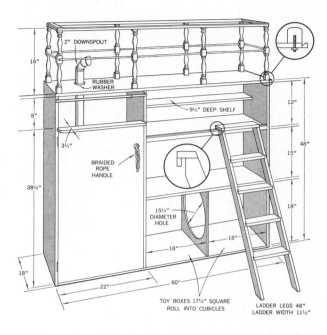

BIG BLOCK *is toy box with insert bottom to hide wheels, is stored in cupboard. Cubicle edges are beveled so boxes roll in.*

PERISCOPE *has glued mirrors at elbow, bottom, viewing hole in side.*

Pine blocks for building

For young boys who like to build things, this fort can easily be put together with a set of pine blocks. Cut 1 by 4 pine boards into 3½-inch and 6-inch blocks. Drill ¼-inch holes right through the thickness of each block, ½ inch in from each corner and in the middle. Drill a matching pair of ½-inch-deep holes in each end and one in the middle of each side. Sand the edges and corners of the blocks so they'll be smooth and rounded.

Make connecting pieces of ¼-inch-diameter dowels cut into 2-inch lengths. The soldiers and cannons are ¾-inch dowels, 2 inches long, with a hole in each end and the side.

For this set, 25 blocks (15 large, 10 small) were used. Extras, with or without holes, can be cut to increase the size of the set.

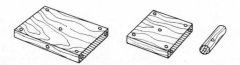

COMPLETED FORT *is ready for battle. Flagpoles and pikes are ¼-inch dowels of various lengths.*

A wagon for toys and boys

This box on wheels serves two purposes—to transport and store building blocks and to ride in when empty. You can purchase these birch blocks at large toy stores or make your own of any 2 by 3 lumber. Obtain your building blocks first, because 2 by 3's vary in thickness, and you may need to modify slightly the box dimensions.

The four corners of the box have finger-lap joints, which you can make best with a wood jig and a dado blade on a table or radial-arm saw. Or you can simply make mitered or butt-joined corners. Screw chest (flat-plate) casters to the bottom. Make the rope pull about 3 feet long.

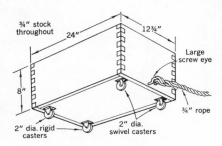

STURDY BOX *transports and stores all these building blocks. When empty, it's fun to ride in.*

Old-fashioned vehicles from scrap blocks

Scrap blocks of wood and various drawer pulls are the principal ingredients of these wheeled toys. Working with a table or band saw and using some imagination, you can turn out similar vehicles in short order for a young boy.

First borrow a library book on old-time vehicles. Using the pictures as a rough guide, alter and embellish as your materials allow. Guess at the sizes; cut and recut as needed. Glue all pieces firmly together.

To make axles and wheels, force 1/8-inch doweling into holes drilled into the back of drawer pulls. (For the flat-bed truck, glue a small wood knob onto each larger, concave knob.) The axles turn inside screw eyes affixed to the bottom of the vehicles, or inside holes drilled through a body piece.

Paint or varnish the toys; differences in wood grain give a pleasing range of tones.

HOSES *on old fire truck are lengths of 3/8-inch doweling. Boiler is chunk of 1 5/8-inch stair rail.*

LOCOMOTIVE'S BOILER *is 1 by 2 quarter rounds; smokestack is wood post finial cut in two.*

TURN-OF-CENTURY TRUCK *uses 1 by 4 pine, 1 by 2 and 2 by 3 redwood. Steering wheel is drawer pull.*

"Anything" box keeps children busy

This simple box with no set dimensions and many openings can be fascinating to both children and adults. When you make it you can vary the number and design of the doorways and use any hardware on hand, as long as each latch is different.

The box was made by first cutting out a doorway in each end piece (those two openings extend to the bottom for variety). Then the entire box was nailed and glued together as one piece, and other doorways were cut here and there with a saber saw. Last, the top was cut off with a table saw, and doors were made to fit the openings. If you use hand tools, it's easier to make all the cuts before assembling the box.

To assemble it, use white glue and 4-penny finish nails (longer nails may protrude into the doorways). Tack and glue a ⅜ by ¾-inch stop strip on the inner latch side of each door. Position and drill lead holes for the hinges and latches, but paint the box before attaching them. This one has a hinged door (on the back side) from the bottom, so it could serve as a ramp for tiny cars. On all hardware, use ½-inch screws.

Hardware used on this box includes a window sash lock, cupboard turn latch, snap locks, latching hasp, padlock, barrel bolt, turn buttons, self-closing gate latch, screw hooks and eyes. Small 1½-inch butt hinges, surface mounted, were used.

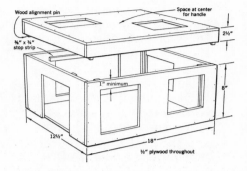

BUSY BOX *can be used for garaging toys, storing treasures, transporting picnic gear, or for just opening up mysterious doors. Top is removable—when all four snap locks are found—for big items.*

Ferryboat does everything but float

Big and maneuverable, this ferryboat is not only a delightful indoor toy for young boys, it's also a good place to store cars and other toys when not in use. The ship rolls on furniture casters and has a rubber-bumper gunwale to protect both it and the furniture.

To construct the ferry, first cut the car deck (top of hull) to shape from ¾-inch plywood. Then attach the two ¾-inch plywood car-deck partitions. This gives you a solid frame on which to build the rest of the superstructure—which can be made of ⅛-inch hardboard or of ⅛ or ¼-inch plywood. Use white glue throughout for assembly.

The horn, centered in the passenger deck, is activated by a wood plunger passing through the deck above. The steering wheels are ¼-inch slices cut from 1¼-inch diameter closet-pole stock and have small brads for spokes. The smokestack and the bases of the passenger benches are carved from solid blocks of balsa. At each end of the ferry are sturdy stanchions for guard chains, made by gluing two ⅜-inch hardwood dowels in holes drilled in the ¾-inch car deck.

The sides of the hull are skirts of ⅛-inch hardboard or plywood that hide the casters. The two bows are cut from solid wood and notched to receive the side pieces. A rubber or plastic bumper strip is then attached completely around the hull. The landing ramps have roadways of 1 by 8 boards; their pilings are doubled 1 by 1's with horizontal 2 by 2's between them to support the roadway. The ramps are raised and lowered by cords that are hooked into small screweyes in the roadways to hold them in the up position.

Design: Ronald Burke.

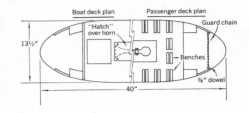

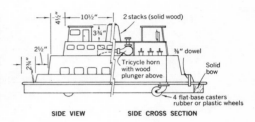

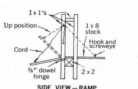
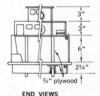

FERRYBOAT *unloads cargo at ramp. Roadway can be any length, but should slant down to floor level at shore's end. Leave windows open; paint ferry and landing, but be sure to use non-toxic paints.*

Play table and chairs that grow

Pleasing to the eye, sturdy, and fun to use, this play table and its chairs have another advantage—their height can be increased as a child grows. The set is made of birch and birch plywood, but you could use practically any hardwood or softwood, including redwood or pine.

You'll need a power saw for the mortise and tenon joints of the sides (to simplify the joinery, use miter or half-lap joints). Make the chair sides and table base 13 inches square and assemble the four pieces of each side with glue.

To form the chair, assemble three of the sides with four ⅜-inch dowels and glue. This furniture is blind-doweled, so that the doweling does not extend through the outer piece. It's easier, however, to drill completely through that piece and just smooth the exposed end of the doweling.

After painting the wood sides, install the upholstered seats. Attach each one with four small steel corner reinforcing plates and wood screws or sheet metal screws. (When you need to raise the seats, simply relocate these angle plates higher up the sides.)

The table base's four sides are assembled the same way, with glue and two dowels at each corner. In the top of the base and in the underside of the table top, drill four holes for the dowels supporting the top. Glue these dowels only lightly, so they can be knocked loose later and replaced with longer dowels to raise the table's height.

Finish with a water-clear sealer and a water-clear brushing lacquer.

Design: Gordon Hammond.

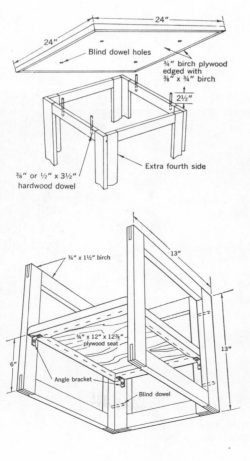

TABLE AND CHAIRS *are useful both indoors and on the lawn. Chair seats, table top can be raised.*

Rocking toys for boys and girls

The rocking horse and cradle shown below can be built with either hand or power tools. The measurements can easily be adjusted to suit your children.

All parts of the rocking horse are made of ½-inch plywood except the rockers and cross brace. Use ¾-inch plywood for the two long rockers. The ears and bridle can be leather, or you can just cut the ears out of the plywood head and paint in the bridle. Optional equipment includes the small plywood horseshoes glued and nailed to the hooves and a rope tail knotted in a hole drilled through the rear panel. Use hardwood doweling for the reins, and bolt doweling and the leather ears to the horse's head. The crosspiece on the reins is simply lashed to them with a leather shoelace run through holes drilled through the wood. This gives a slight looseness in the reins.

The rocking cradle is made of plywood (measurements shown are the minimum desirable for durability). Assemble the bed first of all and then attach the two curved rockers.

Design: Neil Lee.

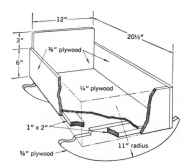

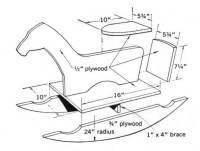

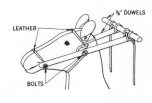

SIMPLE PLYWOOD CRADLE *nicely accommodates sleepy doll. Thicker wood can be used.*

ROCKING HORSE *has leather ears and bridle, plywood horseshoes, and a knotted rope tail.*

A doll house four stories tall

This fashionable doll house has an elevator, high living room, kitchen corner, bedroom, roof deck, and garage. Sized to suit the 11½-inch "fashion" dolls, it can be built in two or three evenings with a table or radial-arm saw. The high plastic window of the living room makes a dramatic backlight. You can buy ⅛-inch-thick plastic in various colors at plastic shops and some sign companies. Or you may prefer to put up a hardboard wall instead.

Other materials you will need are a 4 by 4-foot sheet of ½-inch plywood and another of ⅛-inch hardboard; two 4 and two 6-foot lengths of clear 1 by 6-inch lumber; 8 feet of 1 by 4 lumber; 20 feet of 1 by 2 lumber (or base molding); nails, brads, white glue, and two magnetic cabinet latches.

Make 3⁄16-inch-wide grooves, ¼ inch deep, in the elevator-facing edges of the 1 by 6's at left to let the elevator slide freely. Saw ⅛-inch-wide grooves in the other 1 by 6's and the 1 by 1's to hold the hardboard and plastic panels. For a neat, strong job, rabbet the 1 by 6's for each floor and for the hardboard back. Use 1 by 2 lumber or ½-inch-thick base molding to edge the roof (four sides), deck (two sides), and each floor (front only).

The roof deck is a few inches below the eye level of most 7 and 8-year-olds. If you're building the house for younger children, you could eliminate the garage.

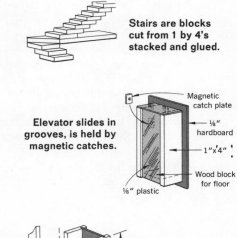

Stairs are blocks cut from 1 by 4's stacked and glued.

Elevator slides in grooves, is held by magnetic catches.

Magnetic catch plate

⅛" hardboard

1"x4"

Wood block for floor

⅛" plastic

Make balcony, then glue and nail it to floor projection.

6"

1"x4"

FOUR LEVELS of town house provide spacious living quarters. Elevator and stairs add to fun.

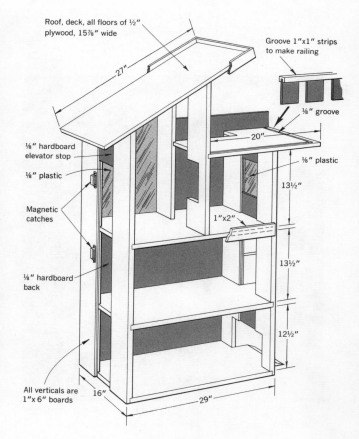

Roof, deck, all floors of ½" plywood, 15⅞" wide

27"

Groove 1"x1" strips to make railing

⅛" groove

20"

⅛" plastic

⅛" hardboard elevator stop

13½"

⅛" plastic

Magnetic catches

1"x2"

13½"

⅛" hardboard back

12½"

All verticals are 1"x6" boards

16"

29"

This doll house can go next door

Really a luxurious dressing room, this portable doll house contains hanging and storage space for a doll's clothes and accessories. It's also a suitcase, so the doll can go next door.

The house is scaled for a dress-up doll 12 inches tall. The construction is quite simple, and if you have only a hand saw, you can make the doll house rectangular. With a power saw, cutting the pieces of plywood at an angle of 15° is no problem. Use white glue and ¾-inch 20-penny nails to assemble the plywood pieces. If possible, obtain a sheet of mahogany plywood with mahogany core veneer (the edges will look more finished). Use white glue to secure the two mirrors and imitation pearls (for the lights) to the walls. As tiny drawers are difficult to make, purchase miniature chests at a toy store and glue them under plywood counter and add plywood sides. Small cup hooks hold the closet rod.

Position the doors ¼ inch up from the bottom. Use brass butterfly hinges on the doors; bend slightly by hand before attaching, as they need to turn more than 270°.

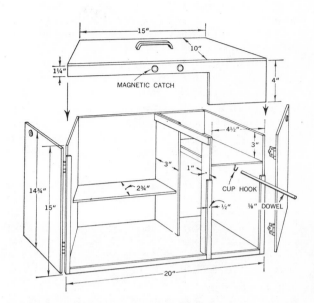

WOOD PARTS (except closet rod) come from one 4 by 4-foot piece of ¼-inch mahogany plywood.

CABINET HANDLE on top is for carrying doll house. Weight is about that of child's empty suitcase.

DOLL HOUSE has wardrobe closet with hat shelf, storage drawers, dressing table with make-up mirror.

Modules make doll-sized apartments

Lightweight plywood boxes (identical modular rooms) make up doll-sized apartment buildings of any height. The boxes can be set together in a variety of ways with roofs becoming terraces for the rooms above. Two or three young girls can share the total set of rooms, each building her own smaller doll house.

The identical rooms are of $\frac{1}{4}$-inch lauan plywood; a single 4 by 8-foot sheet will make 10 of them, of the size diagrammed. You can cut out the various pieces quickly with a table or radial-arm saw, but a hand saw will do. They're assembled with white glue and tiny $\frac{5}{8}$-inch No. 20 wire nails. The rooms shown here were painted off-white inside, left untouched outside.

One appreciated accessory is an elevator for any two-story version of the doll house. It is a simple box of lauan plywood, with a sliding three-sided box inside and a dowel handle.

Design: John Solso of Clement Chen & Associates.

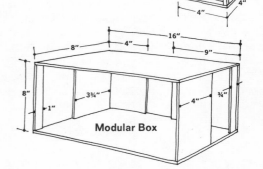

MODULAR BOX-ROOMS *stack into playhouse. Lowest roofs are patios; top roof is playground, heliport.*

ELEVATOR *connects living room, bedroom. Box-rooms are sturdy enough for cat's rompings.*

A Japanese doll house

This doll house shows how people live in a traditional Japanese home. Its large room has *tatami* (mats) on the floor, where the dolls play and sleep. There is a *shoin* (alcove for writing and study) and a *tokonoma* (alcove where a picture is usually hung and some art object is displayed on the raised floor). Separating the alcoves is a gnarled post—a *toko-bashira*—which brings a touch of the outdoors indoors.

The house has a traditional outdoor kitchen (the fenced area on the *engawa*—a long porch—on the rear side) and a "moon veranda" (large bench) alongside the engawa in the front garden. The garden, a tray of ½-inch plywood with lauan molding, has sand glued on. If you use loose sand, it can be raked with a pocket comb. To simulate bamboo, the front fence and moon veranda are made of reed fencing.

The roof consists of two 11 by 31-inch pieces of ⅛-inch hardboard, hinged together with rough sides exposed. Its ridge pole is a ½-inch dowel, whittled at the ends. The shoji screens are thin pieces of lauan with rice paper between. For tatami, a grass place mat was divided into sections with thin strips of black plastic tape.

Design: Robin L. Brisco.

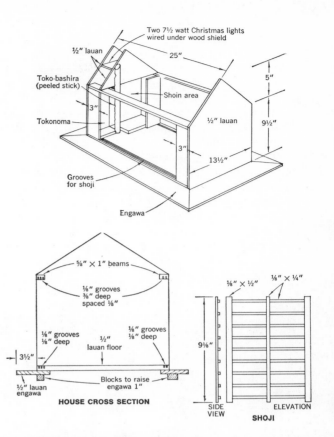

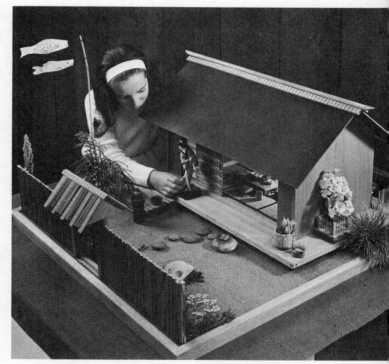

INTERIOR *shows tokonoma and shoin (alcoves at left, right), separated by toko-bashira (post).*

JAPANESE DOLL HOUSE *has engawa, sand garden, "bamboo" fence, flagpole for flying carp.*

An easel for two

This double easel allows two children to paint without getting in each other's way. They put both its sides to use. Each painter has his own set of paints—kept in square, lidded, plastic refrigerator cartons that hang unspillably in a 4½-inch-wide shelf—and a good supply of 24 by 36-inch paper, punched at the top and hung on three dowels. (A 2 by 3-foot blackboard also fits over the dowels.) Brushes can be left temporarily in paint jars, supported upright by the notched brush rack.

The easel's frame is of hardwood; the two sides are hinged along the top so that the easel can fold flat when wing nuts holding the crosspieces are loosened. The backboards are ⅝-inch plywood, trimmed with smoothed redwood for soft, finished edges.

Each board attaches to the frame by two dowels protruding from its back and resting in holes in the leg members. Four such holes running at 2½-inch intervals along each leg make the height of the boards adjustable (in the photograph they are shown 25 inches from the floor—their lowest position).

Design: W. W. Mayfield.

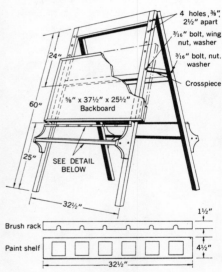

EASEL FRAME *is 60 inches high, 32½ inches wide; backboards are 25½ by 37½ inches. Paper, punched at top, hangs on three dowels. Note brush and jar racks.*

Easel holds a paper roll

Heavy enough to support a roll of newsprint or other paper, this big easel is made from two panels of $\frac{1}{8}$-inch tempered hardboard, 3 feet wide by 4 feet long. Hardboard will not accept thumbtacks, but unlike plywood, it does not cause grain to show in a drawing made over it.

Each panel is nailed and glued to 2 by 3-inch upright legs, 5 feet long, and 2 by 2-inch cross braces, 31 inches long. The panels are joined at the top with door hinges. A 9-inch chain on each side keeps the easel from collapsing.

The front panel has 2-inch-thick brackets to hold the 1-inch dowel that supports the roll of newsprint, 30 inches long. Brackets shown are 31 inches apart and are secured by 3-inch screws through the bracing. (Make the brackets larger if you are going to use 36-inch rolls of paper.) Holes for the dowel are centered $4\frac{1}{2}$ inches out from the board, for a 9-inch-diameter roll. The dowel, 36 inches long, is simply pulled out to install a roll.

At the bottom of the panel, a $\frac{1}{2}$ by $3\frac{1}{2}$-inch board nailed to the underside of the bracing makes a $2\frac{3}{4}$-inch-wide paint shelf.

MASKING TAPE *holds paper to board. To remove paper, tear top against yardstick held flat on easel.*

A place to display artwork

SOFTBOARD BULLETIN BOARD *holds artwork, mementoes. Board runs the length of wall in children's play-room. Youngsters can climb on cushioned bench to hang items beyond their reach.*

Wall ideas for drawings and displays

SLIDING HARDBOARD PANELS *with baked enamel finish work well as a washable drawing surface. Three panels cover windows, keep room dark in early morning, provide privacy. Design: John I. Matthias.*

BURLAP-COVERED *fiberboard doors make bulletin boards. Architects: Ernest J. Kump Associates.*

CHALK BOARD, *bulletin board hang from wood strips screwed into wall studs. Design: Myron C. Lewis.*

A two-faced school board

This blackboard and spelling board set back to back in one frame weighs only 10 pounds and is secured to the wall with lift-out pins. For the metal-surfaced spelling board, buy a 24 by 42-inch piece of 24-gauge sheet metal that is factory-prepared for painting. Paint with white enamel. For the blackboard side, cut a sheet of 1/4-inch tempered hardboard the same size as the steel. Paint the smooth side with blackboard paint.

To frame the board, use four pieces of 1 by 3 stock. Cut to 2 inches wide and miter (at a 45° angle), so one pair measures 43 inches and the other 25 inches. To fit in the steel and hardboard, dado a 1/4-inch deep groove 5/8 inch in from the edge on the shorter side of each piece. Fit the hardboard and steel back within the grooves, and glue and nail the frame at the corners. Set the blackboard surface in the deep side, so you can use the bottom as a chalk shelf. Nail a small piece of half-round molding along the outside edge to keep chalk from rolling off.

A length of 1-inch angle iron, cut to the width of the frame and screwed to the wall, supports the frame at the bottom. Two metal pegs soldered to it fit holes along each edge of bottom of the frame. The top of the frame is held by two pins that go through 1/8-inch holes in the frame and in a 1/2 by 1/2-inch wood strip attached to the wall. Make holes for both top and bottom about 4 inches in from the ends and 1/4 inch back from each edge. Drill the first set of two holes along one edge of the frame's top and through the wood strip, clamped against it. Turn the board and drill a second set of holes along the other side, using the holes in the wood as a guide.

Design: Lorrin Andrade.

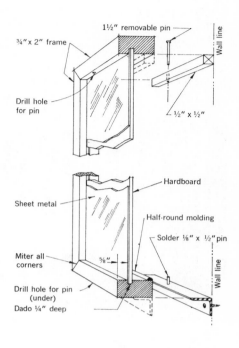

CHALK BOARD is on one side. Two sides are held in groove routed around inside of frame.

PAINTED SHEET METAL on other side holds magnetized letters sold in most variety stores.

Indoor exercise on rainy days

Youngsters need exercise and a release for excess energy when they are cooped up indoors for days during inclement weather. Equipment for physical activity for the home can be very simple and inexpensive. At sporting goods stores, you'll find chinning bars to clamp in a doorway, rope ladders to hang in various ways, table tennis outfits to set up quickly, or, for less strenuous activity, indoor horseshoes and darts.

DARTBOARD *is mounted on cork to catch stray darts. Barbells are for more strenuous exercise.*

LONG CLIMBING ROPE *with wooden spools is anchored to ceiling above staircase landing.*

CHINNING BAR *for children fits in alcove off stairway. Dowel on wall serves as step to bar.*

Household safety tips

PEG *drilled in shelf fits snugly into wood block secured to door, making cabinet toddler-proof.*

ACRYLIC PLASTIC PANEL, *bolted to railing balusters, prevents falls. Architect: John Case Hansen.*

METAL PIN *fits through hole into door to lock medicine cabinet. Pin is cut to fit flush with top of shelf so it cannot be lifted out with fingers. Small magnet, kept elsewhere, pulls it up easily.*

For information on this project, see page 66.

Play Yards

Your child's play yard can be as simple or as elaborate as you wish. It can be a small section equipped with just a sandbox, a corner with a swing set, or a sizeable area complete with a playhouse. And if your yard has a suitable tree, your child can have his own tree house. (A word of caution concerning tree houses—be sure to check with your local building inspector concerning legal codes.)

When planning the play area, carefully consider the surfacing material. Using more than one kind may be necessary. A soft material is best under gym sets and swings, while a harder surface is needed for tricycles, scooters, and other small-wheeled vehicles. (If you have a concrete area, patterns for shuffleboard, hopscotch, or marbles can be marked off with an acid stain. If permanency is not desired, use a rubber base paint.)

■ Fir bark is a popular play surface material. It serves as a soft resilient buffer, safely breaking children's falls. One yard covers 100 square feet to a depth of 3 inches. However, it is wise to have 5 or 6 inches under play equipment such as a swing or large slide. Keep the fir bark slightly moist at all times by sprinkling lightly with a hose; otherwise it will dry out and be blown about by the wind. It scuffs easily and should be raked occasionally; if foot traffic is heavy, the bark will have to be refurbished or replaced every two or three years.

■ Smooth gravel (1/2 to 3/4-inch pebbles) is less expensive than fir bark and requires little or no upkeep. A 3-ton load will cover an area of about 200 square feet to a depth of about 3 inches—the proper depth for easy footing. For neatness, surround the pebble area with edgings that are raised slightly to keep pebbles in bounds. Drainage is no problem—it dries within minutes after a rain. Although smooth gravel will "give" just enough when a child falls on it, it does scrape the skin.

■ Sand is perhaps the safest of all play surfaces as it is next to impossible for a child to injure himself if there are several inches of sand to break his fall. Use it liberally— a depth of 12 inches is not too much. If you decide on sand, remember that it can be easily brought into the house in shoes, pockets, or hair.

■ Grass works well as a play surface, but be sure to choose one of the hardy mixtures rather than the fine-bladed bent grasses which require constant care. Avoid mixtures that include clover, as it attracts bees. Alta (Kentucky 31) or Meadow fescues are durable grasses. In a mild-climate area, one of the zoysias or Bermudas can be grown. St. Augustine is very rugged, but because of its coarse texture, it has to be cut with a power mower.

■ Crushed walnut shells are sold by processors in the fall in areas where walnuts are grown commercially. Surprisingly, they are not too sharp for a play area and do not hurt young bare feet. The shells dry quickly after a rain, are resilient enough to cushion falls, and do not blow around. They seem to prevent almost all weed growth, eliminating the need for treatment of the soil beneath. Their tan to dark brown color is unobtrusive.

Railroad ties frame sandboxes

SPACIOUS SANDBOX *holds several children, lots of toys. It is bordered by railroad ties stacked two high; upper and lower ties lap in opposite directions at corners. Architect: Myron C. Lewis.*

CORNER SANDBOX *is set off from rest of play yard by railroad ties. Design: Carol Wieting.*

RAILROAD TIES *are sandbox walls. Adjoining patio consists of ties framing bricks set in sand.*

Sandboxes can be almost anywhere

SHINGLED ROOF *over generous sandbox permits play to go on even when it drizzles. Basic framework could be enclosed to make a playhouse when the children grow older. Design: S. M. Wetherald.*

TWO CONCRETE SLABS *in patio were omitted; section was filled with sand for play area.*

CIRCULAR SANDBOX *is framed in a square of paving. Landscape architects: Chaffee-Zumwalt.*

Sandboxes hold play equipment

CENTRAL TABLE *in sandbox is for play projects. Before filling box with sand, set four 2-foot lengths of 4 by 4's in concrete, leaving about 10 inches above ground. Two 30-inch lengths of 2 by 10's form the tabletop and are fastened with wood screws to two short crosspieces which are secured to the posts with screws.*

SHIP'S POLE *rises from sandbox. Design: Bettler Baldwin, Owen Peters.*

POWER POLE SECTIONS *are set 12 inches deep with concrete around base, rise 1 to 5 feet. Landscape architect: John Vogley.*

A bottomless sandbox

This sandbox was not built in the usual manner with a wood bottom. It's more like a wood-walled pit, dug 2 feet deep, so there's ample sand for digging and castle building. With this much sand depth, rain water has a place to drain, allowing the surface sand to dry rapidly after a shower.

Make a frame of 2 by 10's secured by cross-lap joints. Place stakes in the axis of the cross-lap joints to keep the frame from moving as you excavate the sand pit. Line the sides of excavation with cedar siding to keep the soil from mixing with the sand and to prevent movement of the box frame. The bottom is left unlined.

Design: Don Normark.

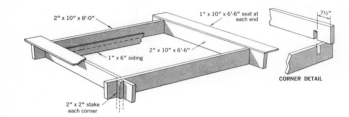

2" x 10" x 8'-0"
1" x 10" x 6'-6" seat at each end
7½"
2" x 10" x 6'-6"
1" x 6" siding
CORNER DETAIL
2" x 2" stake each corner

STAKES *in axis of cross-lap joints secure frame in place while sand pit is being excavated.*

COMPLETED SANDBOX *holds 1½ yards of sand. Stakes in corners will be cut off flush with the top of the box. All lumber used in the box should be finished smoothly to eliminate any chance of splinters.*

Disappearing sandboxes

BRICK WALLS, *set on concrete foundation, frame 6 by 8-foot sandbox. Play area is almost 2 feet deep and is filled with 1 foot of sand. An earth floor provides good drainage. Between playtimes, sandbox is covered with three sections of 1 by 2's converting corner into a sun deck. Landscape architect: Ernest Wertheim.*

VINYL-COATED CANVAS SHADE *pulls over sandbox to keep animals, moisture out. Sandbox and decking are built of 2 by 4's. Metal shade brackets, mounted at one end of sandbox, face inward so slots that receive roller-points can face upward. A 2 by 6-inch board hides roller, doubles as bench. Design: H. Flint Ranney.*

HINGED SECTION of playhouse deck opens to reveal 5-foot-square sandbox. Built of 2 by 12's and 2 by 6's nailed together, the box is lined with corrugated metal. Lid is 2 by 6 planks backed by ⅝-inch-thick exterior plywood. Sandbox is situated over gravel and dirt for good drainage. Design: William D. Heaton.

WOOD COVER slides out from under planter platform to hide sandbox and to protect it from animals. Front and rear of adjoining planter platform are framed with 2 by 12's, the cover with 2 by 6's. Top of planter and sandbox cover is 1 by 2-inch redwood slats. Youngster alone can pull sandbox cover out. Design: Jerome Gluck.

Triangles make giant geometric toys

A stack of plywood triangles, some hinges, and a bit of rope are all you need to construct these geometric toys. From the triangles you can make tepees, moonships, a playhouse, or anything else your imagination or your children come up with.

To make 20 equilateral triangles (this number allows for a good range of possible shapes) you will need four 4 by 8-foot sheets of plywood. Cut them as shown in the diagram, then cut 15-inch-diameter holes in some of the triangles with a saber saw or hole saw for "entrance ports." Cut seven 3-inch holes in others with a saber saw or hole bit in a drill. Keep them all within a centered 15-inch circle so they will not weaken edges. The small holes serve as windows and as footholds for climbing.

Connect four or five groups of three triangles together with hinges, as shown, using rivets or bolts with washers to hold them together securely. The hinged sections make it easier for children (and you) to assemble playhouses in various ways. Along the outer edges of these hinged sections and on all three sides of the others, drill ⅝-inch holes (1 inch back for strength) so they can be lashed together with short pieces of nylon rope.

Design: Nelson Van Judah.

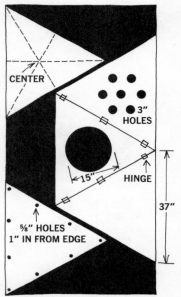

THREE TRIANGLES *make a small tent, four a pyramid. Round openings are child-sized entryways.*

POLYHEDRON PLAYHOUSE, *5 feet wide, without floor, takes 15 triangles.*

A goat cart or a rickshaw

Children don't need a goat to enjoy this little carriage. They'll have great fun simply pulling each other around in it. To make it, you'll need an old bicycle with 24-inch wheels, a chair seat, lumber, screws and screw eyes, and a special long axle that can be made up at a metalworking shop. The basket and two pairs of fender braces with canvas covers are optional. The harness can be as simple as you like.

The rear bicycle wheel has a ⅜-inch axle. The front wheel has a narrower one; remove it with its cones and bearings and replace it with a second ⅜-inch axle bought at a bicycle shop together with cones, locknuts, and a package of ³⁄₁₆-inch ball bearings. Screw on the cones loosely, drop in as many bearings as will fit, tighten cones, screw on the locknuts, and add some grease.

The long cart axle is a ⅝-inch steel rod, 22 inches long, with ⅜-inch threaded holes drilled an inch deep at either end to accept the bicycle axles. If you can, have the holes drilled to match the bicycle thread. If the machinist drills for coarser standard thread, force in the bicycle axles, but don't try to unscrew them again.

At each end of the rod, have a small hole bored at right angles to the bicycle axle hole to accept a setscrew. Construct the cart as shown in the diagram at right; then screw on the wheels and tighten the setscrews.

If you use fender braces and covers, mount the braces so that they are caught between the ⅝-inch axle ends and the cone locknut and buy one extra outside nut for each wheel to hold them on the outside. Each wheel cover is two half circles of canvas, sewn together along the arc.

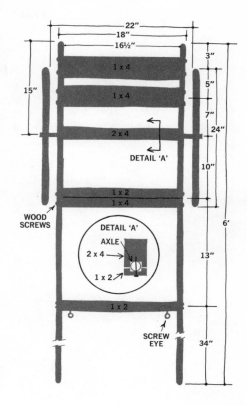

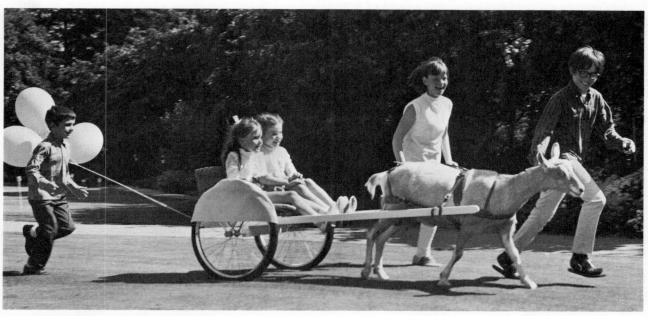

CARRIAGE *can be pulled by goat or used simply as a rickshaw. Wicker seat is tied on and positioned so that child's weight is over axle or slightly forward of it. Fender braces and canvas covers are optional.*

Here you can swing, slide, or climb

PLAY PLATFORM *was made with leftover lumber. Handrails of slide, the only ready-made piece, fit through holes drilled in platform. Ground under and around platform and slide (which ends in sandbox) is covered with spongy bark chips to cushion falls. Toys are kept in hinged-top box at right. Architect: Peter S. Sabin.*

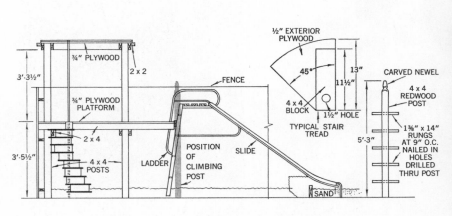

SPIRAL STAIRS *of plywood and 4 by 4 blocks lead to platform.*

A garden landscaped for the children

SANDBOX DECK *with storage shelves continues line of raised beds. Screen at right hides toys, sand from patio.*

SPRING TOYS *are mounted on concrete slabs in graveled side yard.*

EXPOSED AGGREGATE PAVING *in front yard provides running space for wheel toys. Raised plant beds with brick walls make obstacle course for children riding on tricycles. Landscape architect: Mary Gordon.*

This swing is spill-proof

SWING HANGS *in place without nails or screws. Hemp ropes (⅜-inch) thread through parts, loop back up and are spliced in 3 feet above seat. Swing takes following parts, all with ⅜-inch holes: seat of ¾-inch plywood, 14 by 18 inches (glue ¼-inch oak stiffeners to underside ends where rope passes); 4 dowel posts, 1½ by 5 inches; 2 arm rests, 1 by 2 by 14 inches; front and back bars, 1 by 2 by 18 inches. Design: C. T. Morgan.*

These swings are really old tires

REVOLVING SWING *hangs by ropes tied to eyebolts inserted in tire through 2 by 4 wood blocks. Design: Dr. Julian P. Henry.*

TRUCK TIRE *was cut leaving bead for hand-holds, chain attachments.*

Swings that hang from irregular branches

If you want to hang a swing or trapeze from a tree, you will need a length of stout branch that is horizontal for a distance equal to the width of the swing seat or the trapeze bar. The two pivot points should be on the same horizontal plane or the trapeze will swing crookedly. If your tree does not have a horizontal branch, the photographs show two ways to conquer the situation.

The bracket pictured below was built onto a live oak tree. Its skeleton is made of ¾-inch pipes which splay out from each other—they aren't parallel. The pipes are fastened to the branches with deck flanges. For further rigidity, the two horizontal pipes are joined with a crosswise pipe. A stout fir plank covers the two horizontal pipes, and a thinner piece is beneath them. The two planks are bolted together. The two eyebolts that suspend the trapeze run through both planks.

The swing pictured at right has holes, aligned on one horizontal plane, drilled through two branches that form a V in an elm tree. A length of 1-inch steel tubing (thin-wall electric conduit) was rammed through the two holes, which were filled in with pruning compound. Then a ¾-inch pipe, slightly longer than the tubing and smeared with grease, was inserted through the 1-inch tubing. The trapeze hangs from the two ends of the pipe.

TRAPEZE SWINGS *from ropes attached to horizontal pipe placed through two holes in V of elm tree.*

PIPE-AND-WOOD BRACKET, *secured to irregular tree branches with deck flanges, suspends trapeze from a horizontal plane. If ropes were fastened directly to tree, trapeze wouldn't swing true.*

Back-yard play ideas

YARD DIVIDER *is finished with blackboard paint for doodling outdoors. Architect: Robert K. Gordon.*

MERRY-GO-ROUND *turns easily on two auto-type wheel bearings on 2-inch central pipe support cemented into ground. Design: Otis B. Renalds.*

CATERPILLAR SLIDE *is steel drums welded together after ends were cut out. Mouth (cut auto tire) stops children at bottom. Design: Otis B. Renalds.*

DRAGON *carved from 2 by 12 has copper-capped Douglas fir legs. Architect: Robert C. Peterson.*

CURVING LOG WALL *is stockade for sandpile, giant stairway. Landscape architects: Chaffee-Zumwalt.*

EXERCISE WHEEL *is used 50-gallon barrel on pipe axle between tree and wooden post. Hanging bar can be adjusted to accommodate growing children.*

BARREL SEE-SAW *teeters smoothly, goes high. An 11-foot 2 by 12 board is secured to a used 50-gallon oak barrel by six 3/8-inch lag screws.*

A doll house that floats

This doll houseboat is strongly built to take abuse, and when styrene foam panels are placed beneath, it really floats. With a power saw, it takes two weekends to build and finish. You can vary the height to suit the dolls and toy boats that will join it at play time; add a ladder, flagpole, deck chairs, and other accessories as time and interest permit.

First build the hollow-bottomed "barge," rabbeting the four sides to accept the plywood top. Cut near and far house walls (¼-inch-thick ash plywood) to the shapes diagrammed. Glue and nail far wall to the base and add the 15-inch-long rear 1 by 4 crosspiece. Add a 3½-inch-square stairway block below the tall window (stairs are lengths of 1 by 4 redwood with ends beveled at 45°); cut and fit a down ramp.

Cut the L-shaped second deck: a 15 by 17-inch rectangle with 7 by 10¼-inch cutout. Glue ¾ by ¾-inch strips under the deck edge, all around. Glue a 15-inch-long 1 by 4 crosspiece on front, an 8-inch-long 1 by 4 on rear. Join deck unit to sides.

Glue the vertical 7 by 19½-inch panel next to the tall window; cut and fit top length of stair ramp. Bevel (to match the roof angle) three 15-inch-long ¾ by 1½-inch strips to make the basic roof framing; affix with wood screws. Glue ¾ by ¾-inch stiffener strips to all other top edges. Build in the optional front cabin. Add the U-shaped center wall next to the stair top.

Add stanchions (¾ by ¾ by 5 inches; ¼-inch rope holes) and other accessories. Complete painting and finishing. Cut roof panels of ⅛-inch-thick light blue acrylic plastic (this makes the inside airy and bright); affix with epoxy glue.

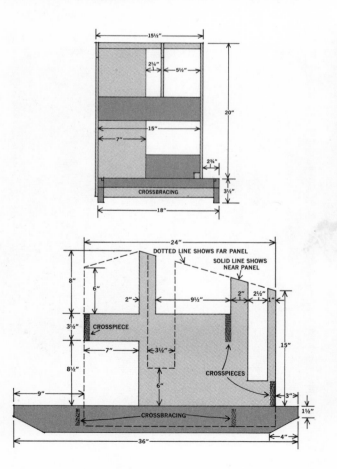

FLOATING FREE *in pool, doll houseboat rides an inch above waves on unseen panels of styrene foam.*

Water play on a hot day

SLIPPERY LAKE *is water hosed onto thin sheet of 12 by 15-foot polyethylene. Move sheet hourly so lawn will not cook; water the polyethylene before children slide, so their skin will not get burned.*

ROPE *tied to branch swings through sprinkler spray, is knotted under seat. Ladder is for launching.*

PLASTIC HOOPS *(cut garden hose stapled to dowel plug) are weighted with sand, float upright.*

An adjustable basketball hoop

Basketball players of any stature can use this adjustable-height basket. The backboard is secured at the height you want by a pair of latches on the posts. At the lowest level, the backboard is held by the lower brace of the posts. Latches on the posts can be placed at intermediate heights up to the regulation 10-foot height. Materials needed for this project are fir lumber, galvanized hardware, and a regulation basket and net.

To raise the basket to full height, just place a 6-foot step ladder under the backboard support and walk up the ladder, sliding the basket up as you go. When you get to the top, turn the latches at the 10-foot level to a horizontal position and let the basket settle in place.

Reverse the procedure to lower the basket. Raise the latches to a vertical position and let the basket slide down to the support at whatever lower level you want. (A more flexible arrangement would be to tie a rope to the backboard support and run it over the top on a pulley and down the back, where it could be secured on a cleat to hold the basket at any height.)

Design: Richard E. Londgren.

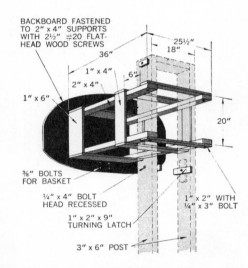

BACKBOARD FASTENED TO 2" x 4" SUPPORTS WITH 2½" #20 FLAT-HEAD WOOD SCREWS

25½"
18"
36"
1" x 4"
6"
2" x 4"
1" x 6"
20"
⅜" BOLTS FOR BASKET
¼" x 4" BOLT HEAD RECESSED
1" x 2" WITH ¼" x 3" BOLT
1" x 2" x 9" TURNING LATCH
3" x 6" POST

LOW-LEVEL BASKET *provides reachable target for young player. Basket can be raised on posts.*

BACKBOARD FRAME *at lowest position rests on bottom post braces, projects away from posts.*

A train table outdoors

This sturdy train table fits 90 inches of wall space between two sliding glass doors on a semiprotected patio. When in use it rests on two benches; an adult and a couple of children can take it down or put it up.

The center well, 20 inches square, provides ample room for two youngsters. The floor of the table is ½-inch plywood, braced with 1 by 1's. The sides of the table and the well are constructed of 1 by 8-inch boards, projecting about an inch on the underneath side to fit flush with the 1 by 1 bracing. The sides and under surface are painted green to match the walls of the house; the interior has several coats of green enamel.

Design: Richard Stock.

WELL BOTTOM *is handy place for dart board. Trains and townscapes store inside table.*

CENTER WELL *brings all areas of table within easy reach. Tracks are permanently attached to table.*

TABLE FITS *against exterior wall. It stores on its side, is held at top with hook and eye catches.*

Places to park the bicycles

WOOD STAND *holds two bicycles, can be installed in soil, gravel, or brick (see diagram at right). Racing bikes take narrower slots.*

WOOD-FRAMED SLOTS *in concrete are 2 inches wide. Form spaces when driveway is laid.*

CONCRETE-BLOCK STANDS *are factory-made, have drainage holes in bottoms, can be moved.*

HAMMER HOOK (3/8-inch) holds front wheel of bicycle to fence post or garage wall. Lifting front tire a few inches releases bike.

SLOTS cut in fence, slat on paving hold bike's front wheel.

WALL BRACKETS, built of 2-inch lumber, hold bikes upright. Long steel 3/8-inch rod slides in holes through wheel supports, and eye on its end is padlocked to heavy screw eye to lock bikes in place. Design: Leo Klein.

A play structure full of surprises

This play structure challenges the imagination. It is full of such surprises as a fireman's pole, a chimney to climb through, and a slide tunnel, so children can pretend it's anything they want it to be—a ship, a ghost town, a medieval castle, the Alamo, or a fire station.

The structure, in the shape of a two-level pinwheel (see model below), occupies approximately 225 square feet of yard space and is less complicated than it appears. Lumber used was construction grade Douglas fir, left natural. For greater weather resistance, you could use redwood or cedar.

The pinwheel base is simply four 4 by 8-foot panels of ⅜-inch exterior plywood. Arranged in a pinwheel formation, two vertical and two horizontal, the panels enclose a 5-foot-square area, with 1-foot openings between them. They are trimmed with 2 by 4's and braced intermediately with 2 by 3's. There are cutouts for viewing slots and a hole to jump through; the designs were applied with a paint roller over cardboard stencils.

The second floor joists are 2 by 4's, some of which extend beyond the plywood walls to support the tack-ons. The flooring is 1 by 6's spaced ¼-inch apart for drainage. The whole floor was built as a separate unit, then mounted over the plywood panels and attached to them with ⅜-inch carriage bolts—giving the structure added rigidity to withstand hard usage and allowing for disassembly if needed.

The ascent chimney, guard rails, and slide are also separate units. All have a framework of 2 by 3's and siding of 1 by 6 Douglas fir. Bolts secure the slide to the adjacent plywood panel. Its floor is made of 1 by 6's, covered with a single sheet of galvanized steel for an unbroken sliding surface. The fireman's pole is a 13-foot galvanized pipe set 2 feet deep in concrete.

Design: Kurt Donat.

First step: Four plywood panels make the basic skeleton.

Third step: Add chimney, fireman's pole, some walls, and slide tunnel.

Second step: The L-shaped floor locks the four panels together.

VIEWING SLOTS *also serve as steps or toeholds for climb through tacked-on chimney.*

FIREMAN'S POLE *allows for quick descent from second-story fort. Note jump-through circle.*

TWO-LEVEL STRUCTURE *is world of make-believe that children can explore and discover. They can climb-up, hang-on, slide-down, or hide-in house-fort. Structure has pinwheel base, Douglas fir siding.*

Loft, deck highlight this A-frame

This A-frame playhouse has a view deck, an 8 by 10-foot playroom on the first level, and a 4 by 8-foot loft above. A ladder leads to the loft, which has carpeting thick enough to sleep on. The loft is enclosed at the ends with canvas panels which can be removed on warm days for air circulation. The lower level has resawn ¼-inch plywood exterior paneling on the ends and ¼-inch prefinished plywood interior paneling throughout to add rigidity to the structure.

The base of the playhouse (including deck area) is 8 by 17 feet. It is made of 2 by 6 joists on precast concrete blocks, with ¾-inch plywood flooring and 2 by 4 crosspieces under the plywood joints. The house takes three A-frame members of 2 by 6's joined with plywood gussets at the top. The 8 by 10-foot house floor takes standard plywood lengths. The A-frames, notched at the bottom ends, are nailed in place against the flooring and checked with a plumb bob. The upper level is framed in with 2 by 4's at about an 8-foot height, where one 4 by 8-foot sheet of plywood makes the floor. One by fours are then attached to the 2 by 4's for shingles.

Design: Dr. Richard Horn.

TWO-STORY PLAYHOUSE *is constructed on hillside. Triangular canvas panel covering loft is removable during hot weather.*

FLOORING *is ¾-inch plywood resting on 2 by 6 joists.*

LOFT FLOOR *is 4 by 8-foot plywood sheet. Shingles are 1 by 4's.*

A-frame playhouse over old gym set

An unused gym set with a strong pipe frame was stripped and used to build this sizeable playhouse. The frame rests on four partly buried concrete foundation blocks. Two 2 by 6 stringers are bolted to the frame, and 2 by 4 joists are nailed on top. Flooring of $\frac{5}{8}$-inch plywood is then nailed to the joists. The rafters, spaced 2 feet apart with their ends cut on angles to fit, are nailed through the plywood floor into the floor joists; they are also nailed together at the top. A few rafters are also bolted to the top metal pipe for rigidity.

Roof sheathing (1 by 8 shiplap boards) is nailed to the rafters and extends over the ends to make an overhang.

Design: Robert E. Watkins.

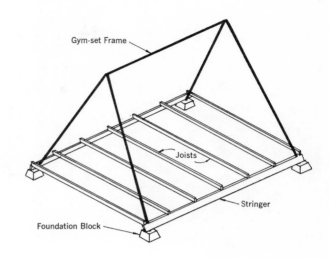

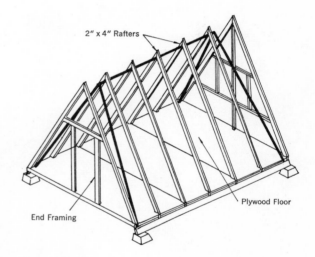

GYM-SET FRAME *makes delightful playhouse. Extra touches are Dutch door and large wood deck.*

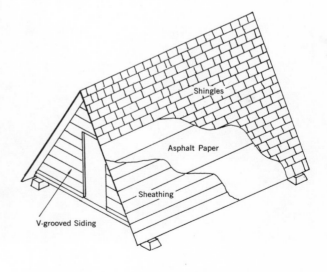

Combination playhouses and play yards

TEPEE FRAMING *is 2 by 4's; A-members are 12 feet long, deck and floor joists 8 feet. Ridge beam is 12-foot-long 2 by 8. Beneath playhouse is blackboard, sandbox, shady place to play. Design: William D. Ireland.*

PLAYHOUSE, FENCED-IN DECK *are 6 feet in air, have two swings, basketball hoop. Sturdy bolted framing includes six 4 by 4 posts, two 2 by 6 ladder rails (anchored in concrete), and 4 by 6 beam. Architect: Ronald Molen.*

Up the ladder, down the fireman's pole

FIREMAN'S POLE *is ¾-inch galvanized pipe held at top by floor flange. Architect: David Klages.*

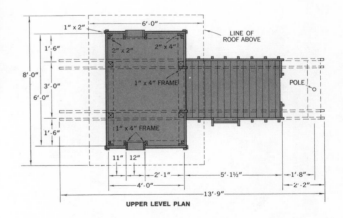

SALOON DOORS *into playhouse let air circulate. Ladder takes you to deck. Lower level stores toys.*

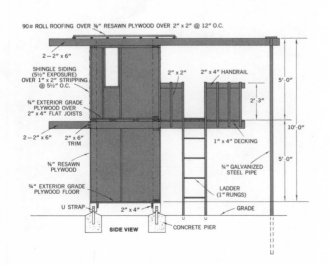

90# ROLL ROOFING OVER ⅜" RESAWN PLYWOOD OVER 2" x 2" @ 12" O.C.

2 – 2" x 6"

SHINGLE SIDING
(5½" EXPOSURE)
OVER 1" x 2" STRIPPING
@ 5½" O.C.

¾" EXTERIOR GRADE
PLYWOOD OVER
2" x 4" FLAT JOISTS

2" x 2"

2" x 4" HANDRAIL

5'-0"

2'-3"

2 – 2" x 6"
TRIM

2" x 6"
TRIM

1" x 4" DECKING

10'-0"

⅜" RESAWN
PLYWOOD

¾" GALVANIZED
STEEL PIPE

5'-0"

¾" EXTERIOR GRADE
PLYWOOD FLOOR

LADDER
(1" RUNGS)

U STRAP

2" x 4"

GRADE

SIDE VIEW

CONCRETE PIER

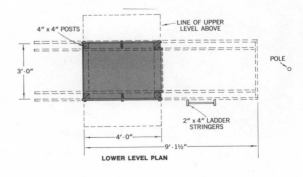

1" x 2"

6'-0"

LINE OF
ROOF ABOVE

1'-6"

2" x 2"

2" x 4"

8'-0"

3'-0"

1" x 4" FRAME

POLE

6'-0"

1'-6"

1" x 4" FRAME

11" 12"

2'-1"

5'-1½"

1'-8"

4'-0"

13'-9"

2'-2"

UPPER LEVEL PLAN

4" x 4" POSTS

LINE OF UPPER
LEVEL ABOVE

3'-0"

POLE

4'-0"

2" x 4" LADDER
STRINGERS

9'-1½"

LOWER LEVEL PLAN

A playhouse for chinning and climbing

This playhouse has two rooms—one opens to the front, one to the back through double, garage-like doors. There's a hinged ramp for wheeled vehicles or just for running up and down. Inside you go from one room to the other through a free-form hole cut in the interior wall.

The fenced-in top of the playhouse can be a fort parapet, a crow's nest, or just a great place for summer sleeping out. It's reached by a trio of permanent scaling ladders that also support one end of an all-purpose platform. You could have two or even just one ladder for less child traffic, perhaps replacing one with a metal fire pole for shinnying up or fast descents. There's also a metal ladder attached to one side of the structure—it's a good escape route when the enemy successfully storms the fort.

The roof and floor are ¾-inch exterior plywood panels. The walls are ⅝-inch, grooved exterior plywood panels applied horizontally.

Architects: Van Horne and Van Horne.

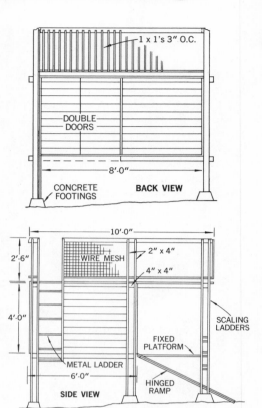

FRONT SIDE *has hinged ramp that can be propped up on sawhorse level with fixed platform at right.*

BACK DOORS *have no ramp, but handy sawhorse acts as step. Head clearance inside is 4 feet.*

Kitchen appeals to girls, roof to boys

With its generous deck and flat roof, this playhouse appeals to both girls and boys. Most likely the boys will climb to the roof while the girls use the house and deck. The playhouse and deck, raised on concrete block piers, fit easily into a small backyard.

The decking and framing were made from an inexpensive grade of redwood. The walls are made of Number 2 cedar shingles (undercoursing shingles). Their widths were varied with a table saw, corners were cut, and the shingles were then nailed to 1/4-inch plywood. The windows have metal frames.

Inside, the floor is covered with vinyl tile remnants; a counter and built-in seat are scrap lumber. Gypsum board, painted, conceals the framing and gives the room a finished look. The range-sink counter is 24 inches high and covered with a vinyl flooring remnant. The sink is an aluminum wash basin, fitted with a strainer, set into the counter top and sealed in place with caulking compound. A small garden hose leads up to the faucet to bring water in. A 1 1/4-inch-diameter hose leads the water outdoors underneath the house.

Design: George Mock.

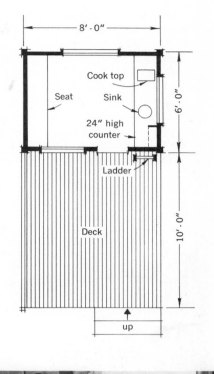

ROOF, *mopped asphalt paper over plywood covered with hemp rug, is good for playing, walking.*

KITCHEN *has electric plate. Sink with aluminum basin drains into garden through rubber hose.*

A two-story playhouse

Although this two-story playhouse is more elaborate than most, the cost was kept down by the use of leftover materials. The structure is snug and weathertight (each floor has its own baseboard heater), so children can play, study, or even sleep there during the coldest weather. The walls inside are painted plasterboard, and the floors are covered with a tweedy carpet. The exterior was stained to match the family house.

Twelve cedar 4 by 4's set in concrete support the house and porch. The framing is fir 2 by 4's; the siding is 1 by 8-inch rough cedar boards with batten strips on the inside. The roof is cedar shakes nailed over ⅝-inch plywood. Flooring consists of 2 by 4's spaced 1 foot apart, with a shiplap subfloor, and ⅝-inch plywood overlay. The ground floor has a low ceiling—it is only 5½ feet high, so grown-ups have to duck. You reach the top floor (the larger one—about 70 feet square) through a 24-inch-square opening on a ½-inch pipe ladder with welded rungs.

Design: Norman Doanes.

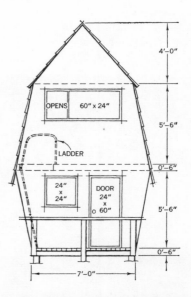

ROUGH CEDAR SIDING *is stained to match main house nearby. Top floor windows swing open.*

WELDED RUNGS *on ½-inch pipe ladder lead to 24-inch-square opening. Tilted wall aids ladder climbing.*

Above-ground structures for outdoor play

CIRCLE OF PILINGS *set in concrete and held together by steel bands comprise trunk of 20-foot-high playhouse. Landscape architects: Chaffee-Zumwalt.*

SKY DECK *sits on 4 by 4 posts, is about 8 by 8 feet square, has three means of access (knotted rope, two ladders). Design: D. James Sakols.*

WOODEN STRUCTURE *has tower, swing, slide, ladders, sandbox. Landscape architect: Roy Rydell.*

PREFABRICATED PLYWOOD FORT *has gun ports, watchtower. Hillside stand, roof shingles are extras.*

A "tree" house without a tree

This "tree house" perches on a pole 16 feet above the ground and provides all the excitement and seclusion boys want in a tree house, but without a tree. (Before building one like it, be sure to check your plan with local building officials.)

The playhouse itself is 7 feet square and 7 feet high in the center. The supporting utility pole, 30 feet long, was pressure-treated with a preservative. It is sunk 6 feet into the ground and goes up through the center of the playhouse, extending 3 feet above the roof and neatly crowned with a metal cap. Helping to support the utility pole are a cluster of peeler cores (cores of logs left over from a plywood mill) varying in length from 3½ to 8 feet. These are sunk into the ground around the center pole and tied together with metal bands. Besides adding strength, they are fun to climb and also keep the playhouse from looking too top-heavy. There is a thick bed of wood shavings around the cores to cushion falls.

Next to the utility pole is a ladder which takes you through the hatch and into the playhouse. The floor joists and bracing are covered by ¼-inch tempered hardboard. Each side of the house has three windows with 9-inch-wide openings 18 inches above the floor. The window panels of hardboard fit against stops and are held in place by spring catches. The siding of the house is resawn cedar, the roof is shingled.

Architects: Hugh S. Mitchell and Gale A. McArthur.

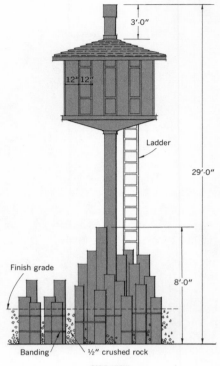

3'-0"

12" 12"

Ladder

29'-0"

Finish grade

8'-0"

Banding   ½" crushed rock

SIDE VIEW

UTILITY POLE *supports tree house 16 feet above ground. Peeler cores are wonderful to climb on.*

LADDER *takes you through hatch into playhouse. Each side of house has three 9-inch-wide windows.*

This house tucks into a fence corner

Simple in its construction, this "high-rise" playhouse puts a strong right-angle fence corner to work as part of its supporting structure. The house has a generous roof overhang to protect the open windows and doorway from the weather, as well as the large sandbox under it. Inside are four bunk beds for overnight sleeping in the summer.

The only access to the playhouse is by a heavy knotted rope alongside the entry. This mode of access discourages most adults, and it prevents toddlers from climbing up into the playhouse unsupervised. The "basement" under the playhouse is a roomy sandbox. Well protected, it keeps playthings dry the year around.

Be sure to check your local building code before constructing any playhouse along a property line fence. Some codes allow such structures directly on a property line, but others require a setback from the fence.

Design: H. Martin Smith, Jr.

TUCKED *into fence corner, playhouse is reached via knotted rope. "Basement" is roomy sandbox.*

A "floating" tree house

HOUSE SITS *about 2 feet above ground on posts alongside "climbing" tree. Playroom and deck are at lower level; big fenced-in deck is upstairs. Upper deck can be reached by climbing tree or enclosed ladder.*

Front-yard tree house has to be presentable

Surrounding a live oak tree, this retreat is basically a deck, 12 feet long by 9 feet wide and 7 feet off the ground. The framework is of 2 by 4's; 1 by 8 tongue-and-groove planking forms the decking. At one end a three-sided plywood enclosure serves as a house and screens the deck and its clutter from the street. With a roof that peaks 6 feet above the deck, its size will be ample for several years. Down below, a broad expanse of brick creates a smooth play yard. Since bricks are laid in sand, rainwater can easily get down to the roots of the oak tree.

Design: Robert D. Wilke.

TREE RETREAT *is deck with two supporting posts and roofed structure enclosed on three sides.*

SIDE VIEW *shows roofed and open-air deck parts of structure. Rope swings over brick play yard.*

DECKS *under oaks need sweeping. Low entrance at ladder head allows for a continuous rail.*

You go inside to go up

INTERIOR *has wall-to-wall carpeting and 6-volt electric lights supplied by automobile battery.*

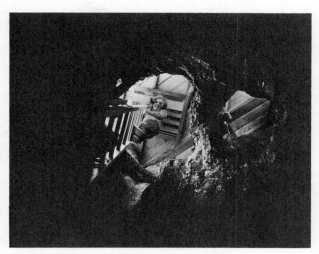

ENTRY *has just the right amount of spookiness. Extension ladder is well secured in place.*

HOLLOW WHITE OAK *supports 11-foot-square house 20 feet up. Doorway was cut with chainsaw.*

Obstacle course for a school play yard

NETWORK of pipes and poles improves young aerialists' coordination. Poles were placed in concrete base. Design: Nelson Van Judah.

THREE-D TUNNEL MAZE is made of oil drums, steel cylinder, tubing welded together.

HOLLOW BLOCKS of steel-and-aluminum, bolted spirally around similar blocks, make jump tower.

RAILROAD TIES, placed at irregular angles on sand or concrete blocks, are securely bolted at corners.

A small-scale Indian village

WOODEN POLES *set in concrete walls make up small-scale Indian village in community park. Variety of design challenges youngsters' minds as well as muscles. Children can crawl through tunnels and under railings.*

LOOKOUT TOWER *rises 11 feet. Large spaces between ladder rungs keep small children down.*

TRIO OF TEPEES *stands beside ponderosa pines. Open structures are made of logs and plywood.*

A children's park in the forest

CARGO NET *slung between trees resembles giant spider web, is popular for climbing.*

PIRATE SHIP *has chain ladder up to crow's nest. Mast is secured in ground with concrete.*

"TOTEMS" *which mark entrance to children's community park challenge young climbers.*

LOG MOUNTAIN, *constructed from sections of old utility poles anchored in ground, is a leg-builder.*

FORT *in "combat village" is made from various-sized logs spiked together so it won't collapse.*

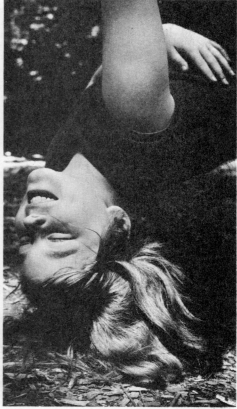

PREFABRICATED SKELETAL DOME, *only manufactured play device in park, is 10 feet high, 30 feet wide. The bars are for climbing, swinging, hanging (see right photo). Landscape architects: Richard Haag Associates.*

Index

Attic hideaway, 11

Basketball backboards, 74, 82
Bedrooms, 6-11, 13-15
  planning, 4-5
Beds, 5, 9, 10, 18, 19, 20, 21, 22, 23
Benches, 9, 16, 27, 30, 31, 51
Bicycle stands, 76-77
Bins, toy, 7, 15, 30, 31, 66
Blackboards, 7, 15, 52, 53
  outdoors, 70, 82
Blocks
  building, 40, 41
  storage, 36-38, 39
  toy, 36-38, 39, 40, 41
Bookcases, 7, 8, 12, 13, 20, 25, 26, 27, 28, 37, 52
Boxes
  play, 36-38, 39, 42, 48
  storage, 26, 27, 36-38, 39
Built-in furniture, 10, 14, 18, 19, 20, 21, 22, 23, 24, 25, 26, 27, 29
Bulletin boards, 9, 14, 19, 28, 51, 52
Bunk beds, 5, 9, 18, 19, 20, 21, 22, 23

Cabinets, 6, 17, 55
Cars
  storage, 29, 35
  toy, 41
Cart, 65
Chairs, 14, 44
Chalk board, see Blackboards
Chinning bar, 54
Climbing equipment, 54, 60, 66, 71, 79, 82, 84, 87, 88, 92, 93, 94, 95
Closets, 8, 16, 29, 32
Clothes chute, 13
Cradle, 45

Dartboard, 54
Desks, 5, 8, 9, 10, 12, 22, 24, 25, 26
Doll houses, 46-49
  floating, 72
Duckboards, 16-17

Easels, 50, 51

Exercise equipment, 54, 71

Ferryboat, 43
Firbark, for play yards, 57
Floor surfaces, for playrooms, 5

Grass, for play yards, 57
Gravel, for play yards, 57
Ground bark, for play yards, 57

Hideaways, 9, 11
Horse, rocking, 45

Kitchen, in playhouse, 85

Lighting, for children's rooms, 5
Loft, 9

Merry-go-round, 70
Mud room, 16-17

Partitions, room, 6, 7, 8, 37
Play structure, 78-79
Play yards, surface materials, 56-57
Playground equipment, 60, 66, 70, 71, 92, 93, 94-95
Playhouses, 80-89
  indoors, 39
Playrooms, 6-15

Railing guards, 20, 21, 55
Railroad ties, 58, 92
Rickshaw, 65
Rocking toys, 45
Room dividers, 6, 7, 8, 37
Rope ladders, 54, 66, 87

Safety tips, 55
Sand, for play yards, 57
Sandboxes, 58-63, 66, 67, 82, 87, 89
See-saw, 71
Slides, 66, 70, 87
Slot cars, 35
Spelling board, 53
Stairs, spiral, 12, 66

Storage
  bedding, 20
  bins, 7, 15, 30, 31, 66
  boxes, 26, 27, 36-38, 39
  cabinets, 6, 17
  chests, 9, 30, 31
  closets, 8, 16-17, 29, 32
  decorative, 33
  drawers, 10, 14, 21, 24, 29, 30, 31, 32
  general, 5
  outdoor, 66, 67, 83
  shelves, 6, 7, 8, 10, 12, 14, 16-17, 20, 25, 26, 27, 28, 29, 52
  slot cars, 35
  toys, 6, 7, 8, 9, 12, 14, 15, 27, 28, 29, 30, 32, 33, 36-38, 39, 40, 42, 66, 67, 83
  trains, 34, 35, 75
  wall, 16-17
Surfacing materials, play yards, 56-57, 67
Swings, 68, 69, 73, 82

Tables
  adjustable, 26, 44
  train, 34, 35, 75
Tire swings, 68
Toys
  boat, 43
  boxes, 36-38, 42
  cart, 65
  doll houses, 46-49, 72
  geometric, 64
  rocking, 45
  spring, 67
  storage, 6, 7, 8, 9, 12, 14, 15, 27, 28, 29, 30, 32, 33, 36-38, 39, 40, 42, 66, 67, 83
  wooden, 40, 41
Train
  box blocks, 36, 38
  tables, 34, 35, 75
Tree houses, 90, 91
Tree swings, 69, 73
Trundle beds, 22

Wagon, 40
Wall coverings, for children's rooms, 4-5
Walnut shells, for play yards, 57
Water activities, 72, 73